BLISS

ONE HERO'S JOURNEY

BY GARY RAMSEY

Contents

Foreword by Colin Quinn vii

Prologue ix

Introduction 11

Chapter 1- Before the Diagnosis 13

    A Typically Busy Life 13

    The Busier the Better 13

    Dark Clouds in the Distance 15

    A Break in the Clouds 16

    Calm and Clear 17

Chapter 2 – The News 19

    A Category 10 19

    The Aftermath 21

    Reality Check 22

    A Silver Lining 25

Chapter 3 – First Hurdle 29

    The Morning After 29

    What Next? 30

    A Moment of Grace 32

    It's a Wonderful Life 34

Chapter 4 – Falling into Place 37

    The Interview 37

The Good News Grows..38

Stopped in My Tracks..39

Unforeseen Support..40

Letting Go Gets Going 41

Chapter 5 – 48 Hours to Go...45

Wrapping Things Up 45

Calming Down Cancer and Death 46

The Day Before Takeoff...47

Christmas in Summer 48

To Post and What to Post? 49

Haunted by My Own Ghost 50

Chapter 6 – Here We Go 51

A Christmas Hangover 51

Preparing to Exit..51

The Final Curtain...52

On the Road Less Traveled...53

A Bump in the Air 53

Entering Paradise 54

Paradise Lost...55

Devine Dining and Beyond..56

The First Awakening 56

The Old Rugged Cross 58

Chapter 7 – Reacquainting with my Legacy 59

    Schedule of Synchronicities.. 59

    Another Awakening on the Way.. 60

    The Remembered Kiss 61

    Death's Power Revisited 63

    A New Lease 63

    Do Dreams Really Come True? 65

    The Long Day's Journey... 66

    Sister, Support, and Symbolism.. 67

    A Reoccurrence.. 67

    An Unforeseen Blessing... 68

Chapter 8 - Hark the Herald Angels Come 71

    D-Day Approaches 71

    The Surgery Zone!... 72

    Is That a Nurse? 73

    My Triumphant Return.. 74

    Angels Unite 75

    Grandma's Encore... 76

Chapter 9 – Making Sense of It All 77

    Salvation Ahead.. 77

    The Past Revisited... 79

Chapter 10 – Bliss.. 85

Countdown to Re-entry 85

Heroic Journey? 87

My Afterlife Rearranged 89

Thou Shalt One Day Die 89

My Personal Resurrection 90

A Dead Man's Epitaph 91

Acknowledgements 95

About the Author 97

Foreword by Colin Quinn

Anyone who knows me knows the name Gary Ramsey because I say his name constantly. I'm obsessed with him because he has kept me performing nightly and away from voice rest for 15 years! A wonderful Alexander Technique teacher named Jessica Wolf sent me to Gary years ago. I had vocal problems that Gary solved immediately. I also had knee problems that he solved very soon thereafter. I continued to work with him because whatever ailed me seemed to mysteriously resolve after a session with him. Even the times when I'd walk out and say to myself "that didn't help" would later prove wrong when I realized his suggestions were in fact working. I've sent many people to see Gary over the years. Being my friends, most were cynics. Every one of them said that he helped them after one session. It's hard to describe his work because it's physical, but it's also intangible.

But on to this book: As far as his bodywork is concerned, some otherworldly force has always guided Gary. That's a fact, and anyone who has been to see him knows this. But this book is about when the bodywork appears to betray him—when he gets diagnosed with kidney cancer. And instead of being angry with the physical body, he uses the experience to unearth the psychological and emotional "body work." He's the only person who can make you hope you get cancer so you can go on an adventure like he has. But that's Gary. He always keeps himself open so that he can receive whatever is out there being transmitted. The psychic connections that he makes and what they do to his outlook are amazing because he already had a great attitude. And he never gets sanctimonious. Gary even says in this book that some of his friends are amazed and inspired by what he experiences, and some think it's bullshit. How could you not love a guy who says that? He can speak like that because Gary is never trying to sell you on anything. He has something of value, and if you want it, he'll give it with his whole heart. If you don't, he shrugs and accepts that. I've run into people over the years who were his students, and whenever we realize we both worked with Gary, we let out yells of joy. Occasionally, you are lucky enough in life to run into somebody who was born to do what they are doing, and it fills you up that you have the privilege and timing that allowed you to watch them do it. A singer, a boxer, a nurse, a fireman—and in Gary's case—a healer, or maybe a messenger to teach you how to self heal? Whatever. I love him. And so does everybody who knows him for more than an hour. So enjoy this book. It's like Gary: hard to articulate what makes him so great, and then it hits you later on.

Colin Quinn NYC 2018

Prologue

When we have been presented with a life-threatening situation, fear is a typical response. It is of the utmost importance, however, not to remain fearful because it will do untold damage to our entire mental, emotional, and physical systems. Maintaining fear as our bedfellow means that we are already projecting a particular outcome and a rather bleak one at that. This will continue to paralyze our entire system and lead us to the very result we are dreading. This is not to suggest that we walk around like Pollyanna with a bright, positive outlook either. The insistence on a positive outcome is just as unhelpful and detrimental as a fearful negative one. Our true power is when we are able to abide within the paradox of the dilemma, not projecting any outcome at all. Only then, may we go through our journey in a calmer and more blissful manner while maintaining our focus on what makes us feel whole and good. If we follow this simple rule, it will help to neutralize any fearful encounters along the way. Remaining as true to our bliss as possible will bring us toward acceptance when the ultimate outcome reveals itself. Whatever the results may be, the quieting of fear and stress will be a blessing either way.

I have shared this secret with as many people as would listen. I have written this book in the hope of inspiring others to connect and follow their inner source as fearlessly as possible and to remain in the paradox between life and death. No one will ever know what the next moment may bring because everything around us is constantly in a state of change. Examples of life and death are in motion right before our eyes as one moment dies and is reborn again, yet we deny this rather blatant and obvious truth about life's uncertainty. The day of my diagnosis revealed to me that there is not one living being on the planet who may not die at any moment. Most of us choose to ignore this reality and believe that something out there will be our savior. The truth is that nothing can truly protect or save us no matter what precautions we may take. Only the deeper part of our self has the potential to provide any solace or protection on this impossible mission. Whatever you want to call this other part is irrelevant, but it alone will help us to walk fearlessly through our darkest hour into the light that illuminates our brightest future. I see this as the sole salvation of each and every individual walking the face of the earth.

Gary Ramsey

Introduction

Since cancer struck in the summer of 2015, my life has shifted in ways that may not be immediately apparent or noticeable. Though much of my day-to-day existence has remained relatively unaltered, my internal sensibilities and desires have vastly changed. It almost feels to me as though the former Gary was wiped away by his deadly cancer and with him, any vestiges of his former life.

The new Gary lives life more vibrantly and has now become involved with a desire to help others who are facing life-threatening issues. I decided to write this book after realizing the large impact that my story had on the listeners of Anita Moorjani's radio show *Explore the Extraordinary* on Hay House Radio. My hope is that through this book, I will be able to give comfort and support to many more. I would also like to spread the message that each of us already contains all the resources necessary to fulfill our greatest evolution.

This book captures the essence of one of the most pivotal moments of my life. Understandably, we can often feel overwhelmed by moments such as these or even left in a state of incapacitating despair. I discovered quite by accident, however, that by remaining as present and emotionally neutral to these events as they unfolded, it forced me to take a more serious look at my relationship to them. This in turn had a profound affect on how I perceived them and participated with them. I also found out that writing gave me a fuller and deeper understanding of my dire situation and beyond it, as well as bringing me greater comfort that strengthened my confidence as I continued on my path.

Even with all these solid foundations for support, we can still become unsettled and fearful as the waves of harsh reality hit with greater force. Staying on course through these challenges is key, especially when the manifestation of our reality is being pushed to the outer limits. This was the predicament I found myself in, and there were not many options available to find my way back to safe shores. Through it all, I could clearly sense that something unique was taking place, and that I was in some strange way slipping through the eye of the needle.

All of us have experienced these earth-shattering times in our lives—those moments when everything that we once thought we knew and understood has been turned upside down. The world that I entered at my journey's birth felt as though I was living in a macabre dream filled with confusion and chaos that was secretly woven from love and compassion. Countless times during and after this episodic adventure, I had to remind myself that this was all really happening to me, or at least it felt that way, yet much of it bore little resemblance to a reality with which I was familiar. The words of

Edgar Allan Poe resoundingly rang true for me when he declared, "Is all that I see or seem but a dream within a dream?"

I believe that this is one of the difficulties our world faces today: Is this real? Can this be true or is it a lie? Should I trust it? I now clearly see that truth and reality are created from within the eyes of the beholder. I do not believe true objectivity exists where consciousness resides; thus, the truth of all reality hinges upon the personal interpretation of our experiences. We can sometimes become tightly locked into the prison of our interpretations, always demanding that they go in the direction we need them to go. I would therefore like to invite the reader to approach this book with a more open and less interpretive mind while travelling through these pages with me. I make this suggestion because I believe that maintaining my own interpretive freedom was one of my greatest saving graces.

I also would like to clearly state that I am in no way attempting to sell, advertise, or promote anything in this book. I have chosen to use the names of real people in my life only as a tribute to them. I have no concrete evidence or proof for many of the events that have occurred throughout this book, other than eyewitness accounts and the fact that I am currently alive and well. All I am attempting to do is to relate the secrets that I uncovered within my own being, and in so doing, perhaps rouse the ones that exist within you.

The greatest thing my journey has taught me is that our salvation truly lies within us and that we should depend primarily upon ourselves to capture it. Deep within us lies the safety net that will catch and lift us up toward our greatest good. There sits the source to all the secrets of our souls. We must, however, be willing to climb out of our accepted daily reality and move beyond it. Perhaps then will we be able to dispel every cloud that comes our way and discover the grace to love each one of them for having ominously appeared.

Chapter 1– Before the Diagnosis

In our most private and most subjective lives, we are not only the passive witnesses of our age, and its sufferers, but also its makers. We make our own epoch.

C. G. Jung, 1934

A Typically Busy Life

The day began like any other. I was grateful that my teaching schedule had settled down for the summer. I love my work as an Alexander Technique practitioner and voice teacher, but I had been going nonstop for quite awhile without a break. In addition, I also work as an opera singer and had recently performed the role of God Pan in "Daphnis and Chloe" by Offenbach with Heartbeat Opera. Following that, I went directly into rehearsal for another project about the Victorian actor Edwin Booth. My only vacation would not be for a few more weeks, and I had to prepare for the title role of Bum Phillips. This was a unique opera produced by Monk Parrots that I had premiered at La MaMa Theatre in New York City. It was going to be remounted in Texas, and I had lots to do before then. In conclusion, like millions of Americans, I was overbooked and stressed out.

The Busier the Better

I had been dealing with a nagging kidney stone problem for years. It bothered me on and off for so long that I don't even quite remember when it began. I was first diagnosed with them when I went to the doctor with a stomach complaint. He told me that I was passing a kidney stone. This was shocking to me because I had always heard they were murderous to pass. It was explained to me that this is not always the case for certain people and fortunately, I seemed to be one of them. I learned to easily identify an attack and drink large amounts of water to help them pass. This always seemed to do the trick. I suspected there must be a reason why I had developed this condition but never bothered to investigate the matter. "Out of sight, out of mind" was my motto! Besides, I was fairly hardy and healthy and did not get sick often, so why worry? I thrived on work, singing, and performing. These were the medicines for my soul, so as long as nothing interfered with them, it was okay with me.

Since I was a small child, I adored a busy schedule. It was my distraction from the world I was born into and my only means of maintaining my sanity. "BUSY-ness" gave me the illusion of having a purpose. My hectic schedule was primarily centered on helping other people. It seemed to be a noble and valiant way to live life.

Unfortunately, it turned me into a classic workaholic and one of the best caretakers in town. I adored these two roles. They always made me feel as though I was some sort of a hero or savior who was making the world a better place. Perhaps my early Catholic upbringing helped this ideology along, but whatever it was, I found it difficult to separate myself from either of these two qualities; I had no idea where they began or where I ended.

Around mid-spring, I was beginning to slow down as the Edwin Booth project came to a close. Very strange sensations occurred throughout my body. I chalked it up to the pressure of the schedule and the stress of the situation. Nothing felt bad per se, simply odd. Shortly after the project finished, however, I passed some blood with what I thought was a kidney stone. I immediately went to the doctor to investigate, but nothing suspicious turned up. As a precautionary measure, he prescribed an antibiotic. He said it was standard procedure and told me to see a urologist if anything else occurred. Nothing did, except after taking the antibiotics, my stomach was not quite right. This was a typical reaction because I never do well on medication of any kind. So, I took little notice of the problem until it persisted. At that point, I thought it wise to schedule an appointment to see my colonic therapist, Gil Jacobs.

For years, I have been seeing Gil for all stomach-related issues. I initially found him after a long bout of intestinal problems that persisted for months without relief. None of my doctors at the time were able to help me. I was tested for everything under the sun and had been given a multitude of prescriptions that only seemed to make things worse. In despair, I took a more holistic approach and found Gil. He saved the day and became one of my primary "go to" people from that point onwards. So, it was logical that I pay him a visit.

After the treatment, he recommended that it might be wise to cut processed sugar out of my diet. This was an unusual piece of advice for him to give. He was not one to make these kinds of suggestions. He said that processed sugar could cause a myriad of problems, particularly with the digestion system. He mentioned that there is a ton of processed sugar hidden in our food chain and that detoxifying my body from sugar could perhaps rid me of the problem. It made good sense, and I agreed that it was worth a try. Although I was not in the habit of ingesting large amounts of sugar, I was ignorant to the concept of "hidden" sugars. The more I investigated the matter, the more I found. I became excited and pumped about cutting my sugar intake. I even hoped that perhaps this would not only cure my stomach ailment but possibly lead to a kidney stone solution as well.

I did not realize, however, how difficult this diet would be to follow. Nearly everything that is processed is filled with some form of sugar. It was hard to wrap my head around this. Many foods do in fact break down into sugar, but I learned that how they do this process is of the greatest importance. Some foods do it more slowly while others do it more quickly. In time, I got the knack of the diet and began having symptoms of sugar withdrawal. I cannot say that they were very intense, but after a few days, I could feel cravings for processed food. My determination managed to carry me through and I courageously marched forward with the diet.

Dark Clouds in the Distance

Within two weeks, I began to lose weight and was feeling great. I had never followed this type of dietary regiment and did not know what to expect. Whenever I diet, however, I generally lose weight rather quickly. I also exercise 4–5 days per week, so I am sure this helped to accelerate things. I had more energy, vitality, and was looking like a younger version of myself. All was well, and everything felt completely normal. By week three, the weight loss suddenly accelerated and no matter how much I ate, I continued to drop in weight. On the very day I realized that something must be wrong, I passed a tiny clump of blood in my urine. I was in shock. What did this mean? I had no idea. I quickly got a good recommendation for a urologist and set up an appointment.

I made my way to the doctor's office and entered with confidence that all would be well. I have lived a relatively decent lifestyle and was not in the habit of worrying about my health nor was I about to begin. The visit was pretty routine and ended with a prostate examination. Afterwards, I immediately felt that something was not right. By the time I gave a urine sample, blood was visibly present. This came as a shock to me, but the doctor did not seem overly concerned. His casual reaction allowed me to remain relatively centered. I thought perhaps it was some sort of infection or another stone. I had no idea. The doctor wrote me three prescriptions: one for blood and urine tests, another for a CAT scan, and the third for an antibiotic. I left his office concerned and a bit confused but determined to do as I was told.

By the time I arrived home, I was unable to urinate at all. There was a mounting pain and pressure in the lower abdomen and bladder. I called the doctor immediately. He said the pain would probably subside and that if it didn't, I was to go to the emergency room. I was in total shock by all of this. Prior to the examination, I felt fine. I knew that a trip to the emergency room would make for a very long and tedious night. In desperation, I decided to fill the prescription and take the antibiotic in the hope that this was an infection. I was praying that it would work some sort of miracle. It was getting late and the closest pharmacy was too far to walk to in my condition. I called my dear friend and downstairs neighbor, Mary Minkowski. Luckily, she was home and agreed to fill the prescription. By the time she returned with it, I was in dire pain. Within minutes after swallowing the pill, my pain subsided. I was surprised at the speed with which the pressure and pain went away.

Just as I had hoped, the effect of the antibiotic was nearly instantaneous. Although some traces of blood still appeared in the urine, I felt great once again. Why? What in God's name was this? Was it something very serious? If so, how serious could it be if the antibiotic resolved the issue so quickly? There seemed to be no logical explanation. I would come to find out later that it truly was a mystery because the antibiotic could never have resolved the issue. For whatever reason, everything had mysteriously disappeared. I vowed to take all the prescribed tests and find out what this was all about. I went to sleep, feeling somewhat calmer and happy that I did not end up in the emergency room. I was proud of myself for remaining calm, and I was grateful that at least for now, all was well. I slept quite soundly.

A Break in the Clouds

I went on with life as usual while making the arrangements for the prescribed tests. This took some fancy footwork on my part because (here comes the big one folks) I do not carry health insurance.

My decision to stop my health insurance plan began well over twenty years ago. At the time, I was paying ridiculously high premiums for insurance that I never used. I also generally liked to take a more holistic and homeopathic approach to my health issues. These kinds of treatments were never covered by my plan (nor any other that existed at the time). Plus, the yearly deductible was higher than the money I ever spent within one year. In the end, it seemed a total waste of money and of no benefit to me.

I decided to take matters into my own hands. I cancelled my insurance and put the amount of my monthly premium ($500) into a personal savings account. This money was strictly "Gary's Health Insurance" account. I never used it for anything other than my health and even let the interest accrue in the account as well. I was aware of the potential risk but was completely willing to take it on. I loved this plan of action because it made me feel so much more in charge and in control of my health decisions. I enjoyed not being at the mercy of an insurance system that I no longer found practical for my health-related issues.

After the first year, the $6,000 amount seemed like a tremendous sum of money and by year five, it was ridiculous. Living without health insurance not only made me feel rich, but it taught me an enormous amount about maintaining my health and even more about paying for it. I became an expert shopper for medical bargains when I needed them. CAT scans, however, were a whole new territory and would demand more concentrated investigating.

My first quote came from a nearby hospital that the doctor had recommended and was a whopping $9,000. I was sure that this was an inflated price and continued shopping.

I knew that radiology labs would offer a far more reasonable deal, and I was correct. Eventually, I found the exact scan the doctor had requested at a more convenient location for only $1,200. I was elated with this price; however, something told me to make one more call to one of the busiest and most reputable radiology labs in New York City. They gave me the lowest of all quotes for only $750 and were even in a better location. I was so amazed at this bargain-basement price that it prompted me to practically cross-examine the radiology lab's receptionist on the phone. They assured me it was the exact scan that the doctor required and that the only stipulation is that you "must pay immediately by cash or credit card." This was beyond my greatest expectation and in the end my total bill, including the doctor and all the tests, came to a grand total of $1,145.62. This amount was less than half of what most of my friends pay as a deductible.

I was very grateful that I felt exceptionally well and invigorated during this time even though it was clear to me that something was wrong. My colleagues were beginning to become alarmed by my appearance. There was no point worrying anyone, so I would simply say that I was on a no-sugar diet for a stomach ailment. The typical response would be: "Well, stop it!" I was grateful that school would be ending and hoping to hear from the doctor soon. I finally received a call from his office saying that all the results were in, but unfortunately, he was not; the doctor was away on vacation. Although a part of me was disappointed, another part was relieved. I was fascinated with what was happening to my mind and body since I had gone to the doctor. I was experiencing what seemed to be a heightened state of reality unlike anything I had ever experienced before.

Calm and Clear

For some reason, everything in my awareness appeared more alive to me than ever before. It all seemed so vibrantly alive that I was tantalized with its beauty and wonder. There was such a sense of peace and tranquility in practically every moment. Though I was not certain why this was happening to me, it felt utterly sensational. How absurd that such a mesmerizing state should come at this time of concern. I wondered as to why this would be happening. Perhaps it was the loss of weight or eating a pure diet that was responsible? I had no definitive answers, but I wanted this new state to remain with me forever. It was a blissful state of ease and peace that I had always longed for but had never quite found.

My search for this type of existence had been going on for quite sometime. This was one of the reasons why I trained and certified as an Alexander teacher. The technique centers on becoming more efficient and easeful in our daily use. For a long time, I had seen my body as the instrument with which to play life's music; therefore, training my body to have an easier approach to my daily existence seemed to be the perfect solution. I have always been far more interested in the process of things rather than their results, and since the technique stresses this point, it was a perfect match. I believe that without a good solid concept of how a result occurs, no one can even begin to master one's actions or reactions. My training as an Alexander Technique teacher gave me a better means toward this mastery. Through its practice, I gained greater conscious control over my body and voice and could use them in more efficient ways. This allowed singing to occur as a natural by-product and even became something that I no longer feared or loathed to do. Shortly after I certified as an Alexander teacher, I met an operatic singing teacher by the name of Cornelius L. Reid, who was amazed by the command I had over my total instrument. He set out on a mission to teach me to sing operatically, and I happily went along with him.

What I was now experiencing, however, took me far beyond all this prior work. I was entering something that felt both strange and yet of great importance. I had no idea what would happen once I found out the test results, but I was not very interested in that. I was far more mesmerized by the present moment that I was experiencing and the level of abandonment I was enjoying. Day by day, I was growing less fearful of the road that lay ahead. I began to have a sense that all would be well no matter what.

Chapter 2 – The News

It is during our darkest moments that we must focus to see the light.

Aristotle

A Category 10

On Tuesday, August 25th, I was on my way to the doctor's office, ready to hear all the test results and finally find out what the heck was going on. Surprisingly, I was not kept long in the waiting room. This seemed odd since the room was jam-packed, but I surmised that the visit would be a short one. The doctor entered rather calmly and looked over my file. Then he quickly turned and walked out of the room. When he came back, he appeared agitated and went through everything one more time. He turned to me looking directly into my eyes and said, "You can die at any minute."

I nearly burst into laughter because I thought this was either a joke or I had heard something wrong. I replied simply with,

"What?"

He repeated the above statement quite clearly.

UTTER SHOCK.

"How is that possible?" I asked.

"Well, first of all you have kidney cancer."

"How can you be sure of that?"

"I can't be sure for certain, but it doesn't matter whether you have kidney cancer or not. That is the least of your problems."

Oddly enough, I was actually relieved to hear this statement. It sounded far kinder than the preceding one. My relief, however, was very short-lived as he continued.

"You have a branching tumor coming from the right kidney. Though these tend not to be dangerous, yours has branched in a rather serious direction. It is traveling up the renal vein. Tumors in this area are extremely fragile. At any moment, the tiniest piece could break off and go straight to your heart causing you to suffer an aneurysm. Death will follow within 6–10 minutes. In this event, there will be nothing that anyone can do to save you."

As unbelievable as it may seem, I actually heard and understood every word of his entire explanation. For some odd reason, I remained calm and asked, "Is there anything that can be done?"

"That's the bad news."

This was the line that got me. I was not sure whether to laugh hysterically or jump out of the first open window I could find. I could not fathom what the bad news could be after what I had already heard. I repeated his statement just to make sure that he understood exactly what he was saying.

"You have BAD news?"

"There are only two hospitals that I know for certain have the equipment to perform this type of surgery: Sloan in New York and Hackensack in New Jersey. Now there may be others, so don't quote me."

(So, I am here noting that I am not quoting.)

"Whichever one can take you first would be your best bet. Finding a surgeon will be very tricky, but the hospitals will be able to assist you with that. The whole thing is pretty risky."

"How risky?"

"I would have all my affairs in order before getting on the table."

"Would tomorrow increase my chances?" I said jokingly to lighten things up a bit.

"Tomorrow may be too late; yesterday would have been your best bet. Then, I could guarantee that you would be alive later today. Frankly, I am surprised that you are still with us."

To this day, the above conversation seems as surreal and macabre as a Twilight Zone episode. It fried most of the operating circuits in my brain, and I could not even begin to comprehend the magnitude of all of it. The fact that this was so deadly—that I might not even live through the night—was incredulous to even think about. To add insult to injury, though I live in the most densely populated area of the United States, I had only TWO choices? Seriously? It was becoming clear to me that any shred of hope was dwindling away fast. In a last-ditch effort, I asked the doctor if there was anything I could do to prevent the aneurysm? Perhaps if I didn't run, jump, lift, or get too nervous, I could possibly buy myself some time?

"I am afraid not," he said. "You could stand up from your chair and it could occur. There is no way to tell what could set it off. I am sorry."

"So, this is very serious?" I asked.

"Grave, in fact." he said softly.

With those last words, every hope was dashed on the jagged rocks of my mind. Suddenly, all my thoughts and concerns came to a dead stop. They simply ceased and inexplicably, my entire being felt totally clear and calm as though I had just awoken from a nightmare.

"Could I have copies of all of my test results?"

I am not entirely sure to this day what provoked me to blurt out this request. After I said it, I was completely baffled as to what I was going to do with them. Yet, I was certain that I wanted them in my possession before I left. The copies appeared in my hand so quickly that I was convinced the doctor and his staff did not want me to die in their office. He wished me well and told me to call if I needed anything at all. I thanked each of them profusely and quickly hurried out the door. As I stepped outside into the open air, I was relieved that I didn't have to deal with anyone or anything. I was simply and utterly alone.

The Aftermath

It was late afternoon and the summer air seemed so fresh and alive in comparison to the clinical odor of my deadly diagnosis. It was a gorgeous day and the immensity of its beauty captivated my senses. I ambled away from the front door of the medical facility in a trance-like state and walked to a lovely nearby park. I stopped as the doctor's opening statement echoed through my mind with one word altered: ANYONE can die at any minute. This rewrite of the line seemed to make me giddy with delight. Of course, how could I have been so dumb? There is not a person alive who is immune from this statement. Anyone, anywhere, at anytime could die. I just happened to be one of the chosen few who had been given printed information proving it to me. But were the results I held in my hand proof of anything? In this moment, I felt fine, and I was certainly not dead. This thought brought me great joy and relief. I cannot explain it clearly, but I felt as though I had finally achieved something. Achieved what? I had no idea. This was beyond my grasp. I sat down on a bench watching the trees as the wind blew through the leaves. The peace, serenity, and tranquility throughout my system were simply euphoric. The air seemed so charged with life that it felt almost electric on my skin. I wanted to stay there forever. It was as though I had been transported to a benevolent place somewhere over the rainbow.

Suddenly, the name Anita Moorjani flashed through my mind. She is a woman I had heard of a while back who was dying of end-stage cancer. Her organs began to fail, and the doctors had told her family that she would die at any moment. Miraculously, she not only came out of her coma, but within days her cancer began to disappear while in the hospital. In her book, "Dying to be me" (Moorjani, 2012), she mentioned that while in her coma she had a near-death experience (NDE). During it, she commented in her book that she "knew whatever was going to happen, everything would be just fine." From the moment I heard her story, it made a huge impression on me. I had promoted her book for years and was not only a great fan, but a big believer in miracles.

While Anita's story permeated my thoughts, it gave me an enormous sense of confidence. I thought, "Well, she was at death's door, in a coma, and riddled with cancer. I am doing a heck of a lot better than that." It was true. I was fully cognizant and mobile. I was certainly not in a coma, and although we were both told that we could die at any minute, she proved them wrong—who knows what would happen with me? The thought of Anita had stirred me from my trance. The strength and courage she had demonstrated immediately snapped me back into a more realistic frame of mind and called me into action.

Reality Check

I knew I had better call my sister, Paula. She told me to call her right after I saw the doctor. I feared she might be thinking the worst at this point. Then, I laughed hysterically and thought, "This is the worst! It could not get any worse if I tried to make it worse." As I dialed the phone, I continued laughing at myself and was just a bit too happy to be making this kind of call. She picked up the phone and immediately said, "So what is going on?!"

"It is really not good; he said I could die any minute."

She began to laugh. "Come on, what did he really say?"

"I am dead serious."

Though that was a very poor choice of words, they clearly conveyed my meaning because I heard nothing from her but stunned silence. Of course, her next question was the same as mine had been at the doctor's office: How? In the days that followed, I became well rehearsed on my diagnosis monologue and was forced to do repeat performances ad nauseam. While the gravity of the situation sank in, Paula simply asked, "What are you going to do?"

"I do not know; I truly don't know."

There were thousands of things to consider, and I was not even sure exactly where to start. Then, I remembered that I was supposed to sing the title role of Bum Phillips in Texas within a few weeks. I mentioned to Paula that I had better call them immediately before I became too overwhelmed with everything else. In that moment, I was more concerned about the dilemma the company would face rather than my own. Before we hung up the phone, Paula said that she would contact my brothers and some other family members and tell them the news for me. I told her that would be very helpful and that I would call later.

The call to the opera producer, Luke Leonard, made the situation I was facing more real because I was now changing plans. Dialing his number, I couldn't help but wonder if I would even have much of a future ever again. While the line rang, I remembered how much this particular project meant to me. Mr. Bum Phillips was a famous figure in American football, and I had been cast to play him just days before he passed away. The opera premiered in New York City at the legendary La MaMa Theatre, and the New York Times deemed my performance a "tour de force." I had the honor and privilege of performing in front of many of Bum's former football players including his son, football coach Wade Phillips. NFL Films even documented the entire process and ran a special clip on its sports channel.

PHOTO 1: "BUM PHILLIPS" COREY TORPIE PHOTOGRAPHY, COURTESY OF MONK PARROTS, INC.

When I broke the news to Luke, I heard nothing but the same stunned silence I had received from my sister. I would become very well acquainted with this particular response in the days to come. I let him know how truly sorry I was for not being able to do the performances in Texas. After a few moments, he blessed me and stated that he knew I would be just fine. He said that he would break the news to the entire team and wanted me to know that they would all be behind me. I thanked him for his kind and lovely words. These would be some of the last kind and gentle words I would receive in the days to come. I wished him and everyone connected to the production the very best. As I hung up with him, I felt more sadness over the opera than I did about anything else that day. I marveled over why I continued to feel so good. Was I simply in denial? My mind was still calm, and I continued to be immersed in a feeling of bliss.

PHOTO 2: "Bum Phillips" Corey Torpie Photography, Courtesy of Monk Parrots, Inc.

A Silver Lining

As soon as I put the key in my front door lock, Farrah Fawcett flashed into my head. She had died awhile back, and I remembered that prior to her death, she had been flown to Germany. I was puzzled by this action at the time until a friend of mine mentioned that Germany had the top cancer treatments in the world. I wondered if perhaps they had something that could help me out? I had nothing to lose except for my life, and that already hung in the balance, so I flew upstairs to get online. I was not sure where to start and simply entered different phrases in Google. I finally found some clinics in Germany when suddenly something popped up on the right side of the screen that caught my eye. It was a gorgeous picture of what looked like a white palace, and I caught the word "clinic." I had no idea what it was about but clicked on the photo to open the website. There sat this white palace surrounded by water in an exotic tropical setting. As soon as I saw it, I said aloud, "Now that is a place to die for!" It was simply magnificent.

My investigation revealed that it was a fully equipped medical center in Mexico. I found out that they also dealt with many kinds of serious conditions and diseases including cancer. The more I read, the more I had a powerful feeling that this was it! As insane as it may sound, I just knew that I was meant to be there. I did not know how or why I knew it, but I just knew it. The facility was in a gorgeous and pristine environment right by the ocean and employed both holistic and conventional medicine. What could be bad? The more I read, the more excited I became, and my mind was swirling with so much excitement that I could no longer contain myself. I had to get someone on the phone and speak to a live person.

A lovely woman named Michelle answered the phone. I wasted no time and cut straight to the chase explaining my entire situation to her while she listened intently. When I finished, she remarked that the institute did handle many types of cancer and was also able to perform difficult surgeries. She added that they generally use a process referred to as "stabilization" of the tumor. This makes its removal far less dangerous but that the doctors would give me all the specifics at a later time. She told me that first I needed to complete forms and questionnaires to determine if I was eligible to be admitted.

"By chance, do you happen to have your medical records with you? That would really speed things up."

I was absolutely dumbstruck. "As a matter of fact, I do. I asked the doctor for a copy of everything right after my diagnosis. I knew I wanted them for some reason, but at the time, I could not figure out why."

"How great. That will save us a tremendous amount of time. How wonderful that you had the presence of mind to take everything with you after receiving such grim news. By the way, when was your diagnosis?"

"A little less than two hours ago." Now she was the one who was dumbstruck. She simply could not believe it.

"Gary," she confided, "You appear to be in such great spirits. Everyone that I have ever spoken to with an outlook such as yours is almost always cured in no time."

"Good, because that is exactly what my doctor told me, that I have NO TIME!" We roared with laughter!

Once the laughter subsided, we got right back to work. Michelle sent the questionnaires and forms to my e-mail while we were still on the phone. She cautioned me not to become overwhelmed and to answer them to the best of my ability. She also gave me her personal cell number and told me to please contact her if I had any questions. She promised that if I were able to get everything back sometime late that night, she would be able to present my case to the medical board by the following afternoon. I thanked her for all her help and support and told her that I would do my best.

As soon as I hung up the phone, I immediately called my sister. She was as amazed as I was. Neither of us could fully comprehend how I found this place. While we talked, I opened the files and they were some of the longest and most detailed forms I have ever seen in my life. They wanted to know everything about me: from birth to my current state of illness. I was determined to finish all of them that night. Once I was off the phone, I received calls from my brothers and their families. I assured them that all would be fine, and that I was developing a plan of action. I am sure they thought I must have been insane because I could hear their confusion and disbelief. I excused myself by saying I needed to get back to work on my plan.

After diligently filling out questionnaires for what seemed to be hours, it occurred to me to contact my colleague Colleen Wallnau. Colleen is my right-hand person at the Neighborhood Playhouse where I work. I had gotten so caught up in the excitement of everything else, I had forgotten about the rest of my life. I wanted her to personally know my entire situation before she heard from anyone else. I also wanted to discuss things with her before talking to the director of the Playhouse. The call provided me with a needed break from the questionnaires.

When she picked up the phone, I was in a very upbeat mood. I chose to be direct and honest. I learned that this would become my best MO when speaking over the phone. Of course, there was the initial shock, but as we talked, things became a bit easier. I believe it was my upbeat mood that helped the entire situation. I was so excited that I now had a course of action to navigate through the storm brewing in my body. I even said to her that I was not worried about an aneurysm occurring. I had no idea what compelled me to say this and realized that my zeal over everything was beginning to overtake me. I apologized to her for breaking such a whirlwind of news but explained that the one thing I could not waste was time. She completely understood and only wished she could be of more help. We discussed alternate candidates in my absence and had a plan in place to present to the director. I mentioned that I had no idea how things would work out. "Que sera, sera," I said, jokingly. I am not entirely sure she appreciated my absurd humor, but we ended the conversation on a very high note.

I was buoyed and energized by the conversation with Colleen because she had taken things very well considering the magnitude of the discussion. She was very calm and listened intently, and I was grateful for how much it uplifted me. It had been the exact magic potion that I needed to get me to the finish line with the documents. I felt Herculean as I went back to work on the forms. My key focus was to finish the entire application, and within a few hours, that is exactly what I did. I put on the final touches and sent the entire thing off to Michelle with a sigh of relief. I was elated and thrilled that I had followed my instincts and now had a working plan in place. Exhausted from the day's events, I had no other choice but to retire to my bed. As I lay there, I still could not believe the roller coaster I had been on all day. I had no idea how or when this ride was going to end, and contemplating it was too overwhelming. Somehow between my dismal diagnosis and my relief plan, I managed to fall into a very deep and peaceful sleep.

Chapter 3 – First Hurdle

It takes a great deal of bravery to stand up to our enemies, but just as much to stand up to our friends.

— *J.K. Rowling, Harry Potter & the Sorcerer's Stone*

The Morning After

I woke up in disbelief about everything that had occurred the day before. It seemed as though it had only been a dream. Slowly, as I sobered up to my new reality, I clearly realized that I was "not in Kansas anymore;" however, I was comforted by the fact that I was still here and not over there. I had yet another day to see if I could beat the odds. I sensed a delight in the developing competition between death and me. At times, I felt like I was a contender on an advanced game show where winner takes all and loser is lost. Though I chuckled about it inwardly, the night before was a big win for me because I had found an ability to make every moment count. This greatly contributed to the stamina necessary to complete all the paperwork before going to sleep. I could only wish for this extra-strength stamina to continue to the bitter end.

When I got out of bed, I Immediately had to have something to eat. My hunger was unbelievably growing more intense since the day before. I blamed this on the diagnostic knowledge that cancer was gnawing away at me. Whatever the reason, I was still determined not to touch sugar and buried my head in a huge bowl of steel cut oatmeal. When I came up for air, I noticed that I had received an e-mail from Michelle saying that all was in good order, and she would contact me if she needed anything else. I was immensely relieved about my decision to apply and to have completed the application. Despite this relief, I wondered if I was making a wise move. There would be no one to count on for help or support in Mexico, although they did insist that I have a relative out there for the surgery. My sister had already volunteered for that position, but I pondered over the risk of leaving the States and began to examine it more closely. What were the good and bad points of this decision?

On the upside, everything would be under one roof with an entire team of doctors dedicated to my case. This would be a godsend. It had been stressful enough running around for all of the tests just to get the diagnosis. In Mexico, even convalescing would be at the same facility. I knew that a hospital anywhere on the East Coast would discharge me as soon as possible because I was without insurance. I would, therefore, be forced to depend on family and friends for help during my recovery, whereas, in Mexico, I could remain as long as was necessary. Of course, cost was yet another concern, but Mexico was a bargain by far even when calculating high estimates. Would the care be comparable as well? There was no way to tell. All I knew for sure was that the facility was built by an American and had been well established for over 15 years. How knowledgeable were they about my particular problem was the question. They sounded confident, but was there any real proof to their claims? Then again, things did not sound rosy and wonderful here either. The doctor had already told me that I might never even make it through the surgery and to have my affairs in order. What If I did die in Mexico? What would happen then? I was sure that was why they insisted a family member accompany me, but what about the rest of the people in my life? How would they feel if I passed away so far from home? Already, the few people who knew about my plans were far from happy over them, and I sensed more adversity on the way. Did any of their opinions matter since I was the key person in this equation? The short answer was no, and something inside of me kept saying that Mexico was the perfect place to go. The appeal for me went beyond logic and into a deeper inexplicable knowing. The more I thought about it, the more mind-boggling it became. Besides, I would have to wait and see if my case would even be accepted. Fate may have the last word on this decision no matter what I thought about it.

What Next?

I could no longer contemplate any more of these unanswerable questions that churned in my mind because I was losing precious time. I had to get to work on the computer and find out how to put my sister's name on all of my accounts. If I died, I wanted to make sure she would be able to handle my affairs. Just as I was figuring out what I needed to do to accomplish this task, I looked at the clock and realized I had to get going. I had two appointments that I needed to keep. So out the door I went to my first one with a woman to whom I will simply refer as Jane.

Jane was an Alexander student of mine since she had been diagnosed with Parkinson's disease, and I was off to give her a lesson at her home. I needed to decide exactly what I would tell her when I entered. She simply adored me, and I knew my news would devastate her. Our work together had been pivotal for her health and general well-being. Although she was symptomatic with Parkinson's when we began, she was now asymptomatic, and her doctors referred to her as an outlier (meaning her disease was progressing more slowly than most). I was a bit worried about what to tell Jane regarding my dilemma because she had an extensive medical background and enormous connections to New York hospitals, including Sloan. I knew she would present very persuasive arguments as to why I should remain in the country. Right now, I was not able to handle any opposition. The situation was far too precarious for debate and my heart and mind were basically set on my fantasy island clinic in Mexico.

When I walked into her apartment, I had a lovely smile on my face and said nothing. We had a wonderful lesson together filled with fun and laughter. She remarked that I was getting way too thin and to stop this crazy diet. I laughed and jokingly said, "Absolutely, this diet could kill somebody." I assured her that I would stop it immediately, and with that, she handed me a large jar of peanuts and made me promise to eat them. I began to smile at the gesture and asked her why peanuts? She said that it was all she had in the house, but if she had a steak, she would have given me that as well. I roared with laughter as I hugged her goodbye, but as she closed the door, I felt horribly guilty about not telling her the truth. I decided to write her a very lovely letter explaining everything and would e-mail it before I left. I only hoped that she would find it in her heart to forgive me.

The next appointment would not be as easy. I had a lesson scheduled with my long-time opera coach and friend Lucy Tucker Yates. I did not want to cancel because it would be my last chance to see her if I was accepted in Mexico. I wanted to tell her my breaking news in person because I could not bear the thought of her finding out through the grapevine and that vine was growing fast. We had been through too much together. Without her, my ability to sing opera would have been a mere pipe dream. I knew very little about music and next to nothing about opera when I met her. She is a musical genius, and her expertise in languages and opera were imperative to my development. Any praise and acclaim I have ever received is largely due to her. She in turn took advantage of my abilities and expertise as an Alexander teacher. I even gave her lessons during her first pregnancy when she developed sciatica. We continued our work together until the delivery of her first child who was born two weeks early and in a record eight minutes. We adored and admired each other too much for anything but absolute honesty.

Before I walked into her apartment, I was as upbeat and enthusiastic as I could possibly be. I imagined that I would depart in an equally joyful manner a short time later. I could not have failed more miserably if I had tried. Almost immediately, she knew something was terribly wrong. I could feel her anguish throughout my entire body as I recounted my diagnosis saga. In the middle of it, I realized that this was my first face-to-face encounter, and I was beginning to have performance anxiety. Everything I said seemed to only make things worse, and maintaining my composure was becoming next to impossible. I had no idea this would be so difficult. Revealing my decision to leave the country did not improve the situation. The entire experience was draining me more than I ever imagined it could. I knew I would not be able to last much longer and finally told her that I had to leave. I assured her not to worry and that all would be well. The frightened look in her eyes made it clear that those words were a waste of my breath. Before I left, she insisted on a photo of me with her two young boys. I am sure she wanted it as a final remembrance, and quite frankly I would not have been able to argue the point. With that, I hugged and kissed them all goodbye and left the building utterly exhausted.

PHOTO 3: LUCY'S CHILDREN

As I made my way out of her apartment building, I vowed not to do any more live appearances. From now on, it would be exclusively phone calls and e-mails. Then it hit me: I still had to speak to the director of the Playhouse. So much for my vow—I hightailed it to the subway. I was famished and stopped at a nearby deli to devour something before boarding the train. While leaving the deli, I noticed my pants were sagging. I pulled my belt even tighter to hold them up and the worn leather came off in my hand. It was the smallest belt I owned and now it was broken into two pieces. I left holding my pants up as I made my way down the subway stairs.

A Moment of Grace

I planned to purchase a new belt before I would swing by work. As I got off the train at 34th street and made my way to the J.C. Penney store, my phone rang. I picked up quickly thinking it was Michelle with news, but no such luck; instead, it was a friend who had just heard about my predicament. He seemed to be less upset by my deadly diagnosis and far more shocked and dismayed at my decision to leave the country for treatment. I had been receiving e-mails and texts the entire day voicing similar opinions.

I politely listened to his argument, doing my very best to be understanding and kind as I stood in front of the entrance to J.C. Penney holding my pants up. The entire situation, coupled with the feverish pitch on the phone, was beginning to wear on me. Finally, he demanded one good reason why I was doing this. That struck the last nerve I had available, and I yelled, "I don't know why I am doing this! All I know is that I am not going to die in an ugly, dreary hospital with everyone telling me what I should and should not be doing. I am going to die in a beautiful place near the ocean surrounded by peace and tranquility. It is my life, and I get to do what I want with it. If you don't like that, then you can choose to do something different for your death; and if I am still alive, I will not badger you about your stupid decisions the way you are badgering me about mine, so just DROP IT."

The silence on the other end was possibly more deafening than the previous shouting. I felt simply awful and mumbled some words of apology, blaming my actions on hunger and exhaustion. I was in total shock over what I had just said and how I had said it, but I had hit upon a core truth: The act of dying was not as scary for me as was the location of WHERE I would die. This concept had not occurred to me until that very moment. Puzzled by this, I made my way into Penney's store and wondered why the "where" of dying was of such vital importance. Granted, the medical approach in Mexico sounded far more appealing and less dangerous to me, but I had not even investigated one single American hospital. I also did not mind the concept of being alone in Mexico and leaving all of my loved ones behind. Then, it hit me like a ton of bricks: The odds were stacked against me here in New York because of my role as a caretaker.

This habit would enslave me into taking better care of everyone else rather than myself. This was at the root of why I wanted and needed to leave the country. I would be incapable of healing while surrounded by the fear and concern of others. I knew all of my friends and family were well-intentioned and coming from a place of love, but they did not understand what I needed to do for myself in relation to this situation. Their upset would only cause me to want to soothe and comfort them and would only be a detriment to me. Besides, all they could advise or urge me to do was based on what THEY would do in my situation. The problem was that none of them were IN my situation.

On deeper introspection, no one knows what the outcome of anything will ever be; yet, fear triggers us into running away from what we really want to do and thrusts us into the arms of what we think we SHOULD do. This recent phone conversation proved beyond a shadow of a doubt that IF I remained in New York—I was a dead man. I would be a slave to allaying the fears of others while slowly killing myself. For some unknown reason, I was completely lacking in the fear department and clearly did not share the fears of those who opposed me. I am certain that the severity and grimness of the diagnosis had eradicated all of that, but whatever the cause, I was not afraid. Their fears were theirs, and whatever ones I would encounter along the way were mine, but never the twain shall meet. I had enough to handle without taking on other people's fearful reactions. The isolation in Mexico would allow me to concentrate solely on myself and nothing else. It would provide me with the peace and tranquility necessary to consciously deal with whatever fate had in store for me. This realization left me in a complete state of elation.

It's a Wonderful Life

I paid for my new belt and left the store exhausted but extraordinarily happy and uplifted. I knew that whatever this journey's end would bring, the results would be mine and mine alone. I began to see how those of us afflicted with illness are at the mercy of the fears of others around us. This not only helps to give the disease more power by weakening our systems, but it can also contribute to other potentially grave consequences. Unfortunately, it is up to the afflicted ones to rise up and face these obstacles in their weakened states. They have only themselves as protection against this barrage of fear, unless they happen to be lucky enough to have some fearless, likeminded warriors to stand beside them. It was clear that some of my warriors were falling by the wayside or missing in action, with only a few left standing. The majority either battled with me or remained silent. Whichever scenario, solidarity was sorely lacking.

This event on the phone had somehow changed me in very deep and unforeseen ways. I felt empowered and fortified by it and inspired to courageously move forward no matter how insane my choices seemed to be. Something big was happening here, and I knew that I had to follow it through to the end. I laughed when I pictured myself as St. Joan who had led her troops to victory because of the voices she heard. I wasn't laughing as much when I remembered how they burned her at the stake for it. But all of that aside, I now realized that the journey was more crucial than the outcome. I was filled with a sense of victory coursing through me. With my pants finally staying up by themselves and my energy revitalized, Shakespeare's line "Once More unto the breach, dear friends, once more" echoed through my mind.

Despite my newfound fervor, I had done as much as I had the strength for and decided to head home. I would tackle the Playhouse first thing in the morning. By the time I pulled into the Jersey PATH station at Journal Square, I had a message from Michelle. I immediately called back, and she told me that I would receive a call tomorrow morning precisely at 10 am from one of the hospital's doctors. She mentioned that once a decision was reached, I should be prepared to leave as soon as possible. I envisioned leaving on Sunday just three days away. This call left me feeling filled with gratitude and relief.

I decided to walk slowly home in celebration of this first hurdle. I no longer felt any distress from the day's events but was instead immensely grateful for them. I knew in my heart of hearts that all of my friends and family only wanted to help. They were concerned and pained by my plight and wanted the very best for me. I was lost in the sheer immensity of the love that so many people had for me throughout my life and I for them. I always had known this but had never truly experienced the full impact of it until now. I had been given a great gift—a kind of "George Bailey" glimpse of my own *Wonderful Life*. My angel had come in the form of someone over the phone. His call had knocked me over the bridge and into the freezing water below where I saw that everything I ever needed was already here. It had always been here in the form of the immense love that exists in this world at all times but goes by practically unnoticed. Walking home, I, like George Bailey, felt as though I was the richest man in town.

Chapter 4 – Falling into Place

The secret to happiness is freedom...And the secret to freedom is courage.

Thucydides

The Interview

The following morning, I woke up very excited and eager to speak to the doctor. I got myself organized so that I could leave the house the minute the interview was over. I had a lot that I needed to accomplish. I finished preparing my list of questions as I awaited the moment of truth. The phone rang precisely at 10 am and after the doctor warmly greeted me, he immediately began to discuss my case. He spoke in a calm and reassuring manner and did not sound bothered by the dangerous and precarious position of the tumor. He only stated that he completely agreed with my diagnosis and that the preoperative treatments should ward off any major danger before or during surgery. He also assured me that these methods have proven to be highly successful in the past.

The treatments would include organic food, natural supplements, and high amounts of heat and oxygen. This would make the tumor much tougher and less likely to break apart during surgery. He asked if this made sense and if it sounded appealing to me. I said that it made perfect sense but asked if the waiting time before surgery would be harmful in any way. He said they would monitor the situation very closely and determine when it was best to stop the preliminary treatments and perform surgery. He told me that what they needed me to do right now was to stick to a very strict diet: no processed sugar or processed food of any kind, no meat except for fish or fowl, no caffeine whatsoever, drink lots of water, and keep everything as organic as possible. He said, "This diet will begin the process of making the tumor work harder to survive: The better the treatments prior to surgery, the better the surgery's outcome."

He discussed how my own mental and emotional states were of the utmost importance and would be major factors toward a successful outcome. He mentioned that he had already heard that I was doing a good job in this area and to keep it up. He asked me if I had a companion to accompany me, and I told him that my sister was all set to join me in Mexico when I received a proposed date for surgery. He asked if I had any other reservations or issues, and I did have one: the flight. I had heard that flying could potentially increase my chances to have an aneurysm occur. He stated very clearly that the diet was the key. He added that cutting processed sugar out of my diet prior to my diagnosis is "probably the main reason that you are alive at present." Though I had always believed that we are what we eat, it never hit me as hard as it did at that precise moment. He promised that I would hear from them very soon as to their decision. "Your case-worker, Michelle, will be your contact for all future questions or issues." I thanked the doctor for everything and said that I looked forward to hearing from them.

As I hung up the phone, I was simply amazed with the promptness, professionalism, and kindness of the call. There was nothing grave or serious in his tone or manner. It was completely free of solemnity or crisis and instead was simple, direct, and easy to understand. Now it was out of my hands and there was nothing more I could do but wait for the verdict. I was pretty sure that I would be approved, but there was always that shadow of doubt hanging in the balance. For all I knew, I might not even live long enough to receive my acceptance. Oddly, I found this thought comforting because it reminded me that the universe was in charge of all outcomes and not me.

The Good News Grows

I called my sister to update her on the interview. She also had a host of things to report to me from her research on the hospital's website. To begin with, they supplied all clothing and personal hygiene products. Everything was completely organic and natural. Their entire philosophy: A compromised system must live in the cleanest, most natural environment possible. I had been so busy that I did not have a chance to read up on all the specifics. Every bit of information made me long to be there instantaneously. I wanted to hear more but, unfortunately, I had to get off the phone and get to work as quickly as possible. I told her that we would talk later.

While I was on my way into Manhattan, my phone rang, and it was Michelle. "Gary, all systems are a go!" I was beyond relieved and overwhelmed with joy. I found out later that, right after the doctor had hung up the phone with me, he presented my case to the medical staff. I told Michelle how excited I was to be coming and looked forward to meeting everyone. "The institute is also very excited about you coming as well. You are the kind of person we love to get." Surprised by this statement, I asked her why.

"Because you have not had any prior medical treatments. This is unusual. Most people come here after they have exhausted many other possibilities. We are usually the last resort." I was a bit surprised by this statement but, in light of all the opposition I had been facing, it made perfect sense.

"We would like you out here as soon as possible; so what are you thinking?" I knew I wouldn't be able to get everything together until Sunday, which was only two days away. I quickly offered that as my first choice. She said that Sunday would be spectacular because it is their calmest day of the week. I would be able to get acclimated to everything and then begin a very busy schedule on Monday.

"One more thing. You will have to fly into San Diego and we will be able to pick you up from there. Only arrange a one-way ticket—do not book a round trip. You have no definitive return date, and the airlines can give you lots of trouble if the date goes long past your projected one. There is no way to guess when you will be coming back."

Here it was again. Of course, how could I or anyone know when I would be returning or even if I would ever return? Although Michelle did not allude to my death in any way, the message was loud and clear. I would have just gone ahead and booked a round trip without giving it a second thought. This wonderful little message reminded me to stay in the moment and not to depend on the future. I would come to find that this habit would become my greatest lifesaver. I thanked her and told her that she would hear back from me later that day. I quickly texted a simple message to my sister: "I got it. Look for one-way flights to San Diego."

Stopped in My Tracks

Right after I sent the text, I looked up and saw my bank in front of me at Journal Square. It dawned on me that I had never resolved the issue to link my sister to my bank accounts. With only two days left, I needed to resolve this as quickly as possible. When I entered the bank, I went directly up to the manager. She was a lovely woman named Connie and I explained all the trouble I had trying to add my sister's name to my account. She gave me the exact same seven-business-day story I had heard over the phone, and I stopped her in mid-sentence.

"I know this may sound unbelievable to you, but please know that every word I am about to tell you is true. My doctors have told me that I could die at any minute. I am going to Mexico for a treatment that could possibly save my life. I need my sister on this account before I leave because if things go badly, she will be stuck out there with none of my financial resources available to her. So, I do not have seven business days to wait for this—I may not even have the next seven minutes. Is there anything you could possibly do to help me?"

These words had simply flown out of my mouth without any thought or hesitation. I was calm and centered in the delivery of them yet determined to resolve this issue. This was the first time I had used my dire circumstances to attain any favor or preferential treatment. She looked back at me with such compassion that it still brings tears to my eyes today.

"I promise I will help you."

With that, she did something on her computer and then called someone on her phone. She looked at me and asked when I was leaving the country. "This Sunday," I replied.

She softly said something over the phone as she tapped her computer keys. When she finished, she turned to me and said, "I will handle this personally. Tell your sister to contact her bank in Chicago and explain the situation to them. Then tell her to make an appointment with anyone from her bank staff Saturday morning at 10 am sharp and to expect a call from us. Your sister will be a joint holder on your account before you leave."

Tears were welling up in my eyes as I gently put my hand over hers and said, "Thank you so much; you have no idea how much this means to me."

She looked at me and said, "I wish there was more I could do for you." I met her eyes and replied, "You've done more for me than I can ever tell you. I will see you Saturday morning!" With that, I walked out to my train.

Unforeseen Support

When I arrived in New York, I called the Playhouse to see if the director, Pamela Moller Kareman, would be able to meet with me before lunchtime. To my utter surprise, I found out that she was not coming in and had begun her vacation. As I dialed her cell, I was simultaneously breathing a sigh of relief. These face-to-face meetings with people were beginning to take their toll on me. Even the meeting with the bank manager proved to be more emotionally draining than I had expected, and I had never even met that dear woman before today. Unfortunately, Pam's voicemail picked up, so I left a rather urgent message. She returned the call within minutes.

I remained very calm as I recounted my entire cancer monologue to Pam. I don't believe she was terribly shocked because the last time she had seen me I was looking very thin, and she may have suspected something. Whatever her prior thoughts may have been, her response was absolutely terrific. As soon as I finished speaking, she immediately stated that I would be returning back to work once I was well enough to do so. Her words, whether they were destiny's decision or not, completely melted my heart. We agreed there would not be a public announcement to anyone at the school. I told her to handle everything in whatever manner she thought best. I mentioned that I had already discussed everything with Colleen who had a list of potential substitutes. I also told her that I would contact the Alexander teacher she had recently hired on my recommendation. She wished me well and sent me her love and her blessings.

I quickly got on the phone with Anne Waxman. She is a highly respected Alexander teacher in New York City who was going to be teaching with me for the fall term. As I dialed the phone, I thought that this could not be more awkward if I had staged it myself. The Alexander position works in tandem with the second-year voice class, and I was so excited that the two of us would finally have the opportunity to be working together. Fate was bringing an end to my perfectly laid plans. As I broke the news to Anne, she remained very calm, centered, and took all of it surprisingly well. She was extremely understanding and supportive, and I very much appreciated her lovely response. I told her not to worry and assured her that I was leaving an excellent list of people to substitute for me. I said that we would speak further about everything at a later time because I had to run to teach several private clients.

I decided that I would teach each lesson before sharing the news that I would be away for an extended period of time. I had made an executive decision to tell all of them the whole truth. One comfort in this was that I was certain not to get any backlash on my decision to go to Mexico; I was one hundred percent correct. Every one of them was totally supportive and gave me his or her blessings, whether he or she believed in what I was doing or not. It made it a much easier day in this respect, and teaching felt good and filled me with energy. In general, the Alexander work demands a sense of presence during the lesson while the mind remains focused and does not wander. I believe it was this aspect of the work that was responsible for my being able to do so well since the diagnosis. By the last lesson of the day, however, my energy was beginning to wane. I could sense a cloud of exhaustion moving my way and I was starving to boot, so I made a fast track home.

I received another call from Anne and picked up instantly, thinking there was some sort of problem. There wasn't; she wanted to ask me a question.

"Would you like to have a session with a woman by the name of Deborah Gill? She is a very gifted healer and intuitive who works a lot with people who have cancer."

Now this is not something that I would be opposed to, but time was literally running out before my departure. I explained my time crunch to Anne and that I would probably be unable to do it. She completely understood, and I thanked her profusely for her kind gesture. The entire day had been filled with love and support from unexpected places, and it lifted my spirits immensely.

Letting Go Gets Going

When I arrived home, I got my sister on the phone and broke down in tears. I was tired, famished, and overwrought, but underneath it all, my tears were filled with joy and gratitude. The simple relief of being accepted to the institute and finally having a plan in place was awesome. I remember telling my sister, "Whatever happens is up to the universe and the heavens above." I believed in what I was doing, and right or wrong, I was bound and determined to execute it. My sister had managed to research some flights. She suggested calling as opposed to booking online to make the reservation so that I could explain my situation. I briefed her on the banking predicament, and she said she would contact her branch immediately and schedule the Saturday appointment. I was blown away with how quickly everything was falling into place. I took this as a sign that I was meant to be in Mexico. I believe that when things work this easily, the universe is sending its blessings.

Once we were off the phone, I immediately contacted the airlines and booked the rather inexpensive one-way fare that Paula had suggested. I discussed my situation with the ticket agent and asked her advice on the check-in to avoid being detained. She said she would note it as a special one-way fare for medical purposes. My flight would take off very early in the morning, so I would have to hire a car. Just as I was hanging up with the airlines, my neighbor, Mary, came up to find out what was happening. I briefed her on everything while I ate a gigantic salad. She was elated with how well everything was going and insisted that she would arrange the limo to the airport.

I was now free to get other things done, and there was one in particular that I had been avoiding: a letter to my client, Jane. She was the only person I had out-and-out lied to, and I was still feeling guilty about it. I sat down and comprised a beautiful and uplifting letter filled with humor and love. In it, I explained how awful I felt for not telling her the truth and asked for her forgiveness. I told her that I did not have the strength to defend my choice nor did I have very good reasons for my decision. I described how I had based my move on my intuition and my feelings. I knew that neither of these would ever hold up over her vast knowledge of cancer. I even said that her expertise would have been the straw to break my Mexican back in half. Toward the end of the letter, I wrote:

"I truly know that staying here would be sheer suicide for me. My decision to leave the country has brought me immense joy...I am so happy right now that it is beyond explanation. Even if I die, I will die happily, knowing that I followed my own heart and did not abandon myself."

I was very happy with the draft and meant every word of it. There was an immense feeling of satisfaction running through me. Here I was, in the most dreadful circumstances of my life, and instead of being scared or frightened, I felt enormously happy and free. In fact, I felt freer while traversing this narrow path between life and death than I had ever felt before. I was above all the DOs and DON'Ts of this world and was soaring beyond the confines of my mind into a new and unknown territory. Writing Jane's letter uplifted my spirits once again and lulled me into the sweetness of following my truth. A poem by T.S. Elliot echoed through my mind.

"We shall not cease from exploration, and the end of all our exploring will be to arrive where we started and know the place for the first time." And on that thought, I fell blissfully asleep.

Chapter 5 – 48 Hours to Go

Your life is not a countdown to your death, but a stepping-stone for the lives that will live after you. Squander today, and you will find yourself useless tomorrow.

— *A.J. Darkholme, Rise of the Morningstar*

Wrapping Things Up

The next two days were a whirlwind of activity. Only certain things stick in my mind because the unfolding of events accelerated greatly. This entire time was highlighted by the freedom I felt writing Jane's letter. Once I had put into words how and why I needed to follow my intuition and feelings, it unleashed something deep inside of me. I had been taught all of my life to do for others while ignoring and diminishing my own needs and desires. This letter inspired me to take back my power and smash this old habit of putting myself in the back seat. I was filled with a fire to follow my quest with the fury of my intuitive sense leading the way.

I had always believed in the power of the intuition—that within each of us, there is an inexhaustible reservoir of truth that helps to guide us toward our greatest good. Having a strong belief is not quite the same as embodying that belief and putting it into action. Would my intuition and instincts lead me in a good direction? This is what I was willing to bet on especially since I had no other sure bets available to me. I was not a stranger to following my intuition and occasionally relied upon it throughout my adulthood. I even found at times that it led me to make new discoveries about myself, which eventually put me on a completely different path.

For example, I became an acting student on an intuitive hunch. I had always been drawn to acting but never considered it as a profession. My work as an actor compelled me to explore my voice and body more deeply. This eventually led me to the Alexander Technique because I felt drawn to helping others with their physical and vocal constraints. In turn, Alexander school was a crucial component in my development as an opera singer. In conclusion, my initial intuitive hunch indirectly resulted in my multi-faceted careers, none of which I would have chosen on my own.

Now this current challenge was giving me more than ample opportunity to put my money where my mouth is. I would need every resource I had from my past and present to come to my aid on this death-defying journey. If I succeeded, I would prove to myself once and for all that I am my own greatest guide. If I failed, I was certain that I would be happy in having made the attempt. I was the compass to navigate through these rough waters, and the resulting destination would hopefully still point back to myself.

Calming Down Cancer and Death

The closer I got to my departure date, the more fascinated I became with the changes in my mind and body. I was developing a new understanding surrounding cancer and death. Although both of them were present at every single moment, they lost most of their power over me. I saw them more and more as my friends and began to live in union with them instead of against them. I accepted all of the changes that I was undergoing and no longer worried about them. My continuous weight loss, bouts of pain, blood in the urine, and nagging hunger now revealed themselves as a natural process of my condition.

I had an image of giving birth to something beyond this tumor. I even joked at times that I was carrying Rosemary's baby. I had compassion toward this baby of a tumor and felt as though I was nurturing it as opposed to loathing it. I was doing everything in my power to assist in its safe delivery. Seeing this as a labor of love helped me to become an active participant rather than an invaded victim. After all, it was a creation conceived within my body, and like it or not, I was bound and determined to bring it forth into the light of day. In short, I was losing my former concepts of what cancer and death had previously meant to me. Now I was putting my total faith, trust, and attention into the sacredness of the present moment. I listened intently to what my body, heart, intuition, and higher self were telling me. There was nothing else to cling to because the past and the future were of no use to me. They were more foreboding than comforting and slowly both of them became of little consequence.

I also continued to capitalize on the freedom I had found by writing Jane's letter and was inspired to write more. I poured out pages of words that would go into letters, notes, and journals. Some of them would be sent, some would only be sent in the event of my death, and some would never be seen. Whatever their purpose, they continued to raise my spirits. I even mused that this new therapy would become my epitaph. I wrote about how ridiculous it was to feel so good in a body that was wasting away. There was no rational reason for me to be on this absurd high. Things were certainly not coming up roses. I faced immense opposition on the home front, and I hadn't the slightest idea what would really happen when I arrived at my fantasy island clinic. In short, there was no proof that my actions were nothing other than sheer insanity; yet, I was ecstatic to carry out my mission impossible. I cannot explain the whys and wherefores even to this day. I can only say that I was high on whatever life I had left to live.

The Day Before Takeoff

When Saturday arrived, it was jam-packed with the final hoops that I needed to jump through. The day began with the bank, and before entering, I knew that whatever would happen was not in my control. I decided to lovingly accept what awaited me. Dear Connie, the bank manager, appeared with a smile on her face and ready to help me with my banking dilemma. All parties connected at the designated hour, and as promised, I left with my sister as joint holder on all of my accounts. Connie had performed with splendid excellence. I bid her a fond farewell and thanked her profusely before I ran off to teach my remaining clients. The last of these would be Colin Quinn.

Colin had been a long-time client and friend of mine. His career as a stand-up comedian is well established and practically iconic. When we first met, he had been plagued for some time by vocal issues that were interfering with his work. Comedians and actors alike are prone to this sort of difficulty on a continual basis. It is the nature of the business, and in stand-up, without a voice, you are not standing at all. Colin was hell-bent on improving his vocal ability in performance and resolving these issues once and for all. From the very first, we really hit it off and have worked together ever since. He eventually freed himself from vocal distress and proved this on Broadway. In his one-man show "Long Story Short," he was able to sustain eight shows a week with three consecutive ones every Saturday. Never once did he experience vocal difficulties for the entire run and from that point on, I was as good as gold in his eyes. He promoted me wherever he went. I even believe his friend and collaborator, Jerry Seinfeld, who directed the show, grew suspicious of this magical Gary Ramsey until he met me in person.

The last time I had seen Colin was at the opening of the film "Trainwreck," in which he played the role of the father, Gordon Townsend. He invited me to the opening of the film, and in true Colin fashion had once again made my name infamous to the entire cast and crew. When he introduced me to the star of the film, Amy Schumer, she went into an award-winning routine about constantly hearing the name of Gary Ramsey. I began to silently laugh to myself as I recalled that wonderful evening before the word "cancer" entered my life.

I was concerned about Colin's reaction to my news. Primarily, I had always been the one to help solve the issues he was having, so it felt odd that I was now coming to him with something so major and monumental. More importantly, I simply did not want to leave the country without his blessing. If this turned into an intense scene, it would put a serious damper on my morning departure. I began to muse how I would break the news to him, and I thought perhaps that I would do it like a comedy skit. I would end it with the joke about the Mexican fantasy island clinic where they will miraculously cure me. To close the routine, I would possibly sing, "I'm so glad we had this time together" from the old Carol Burnett Show. Bad as this idea sounded to me, it was the best I could come up with.

As each student arrived, I was energized and ready to dive into action. I followed my established routine of teaching the lessons first and breaking the news last. When Colin appeared, I felt my nerves beginning to take hold. Luckily, he is always in a rather jovial mood and was making me laugh pretty hard. Amidst the laughs, I finally said that I needed to tell him something. That is when all the laughing stopped. I put my best foot forward as I delivered my cancer monologue for the final time. As hard as I tried to sell the hell out of my routine, he was far from amused. Like my sister, however, he had long learned to trust my judgment and went along with it. I continued to assure him that everything would be fine because the clinic sounded like they really knew what they were doing. I am not sure if he entirely bought that, but we left each other in good spirits. It was the perfect end to my last day in New York. I promised that I would do my best to stay in touch with him. Little did I know how hard it would be to keep that promise.

Christmas in Summer

As we walked in opposite directions, I secretly wondered if I would ever see Colin again. What would truly be in store for me at the end of this saga? Once again, I caught this futuristic thinking and put a stop to it at once. By now, I had intimately learned that any thoughts about the future would deaden my internal strength, and I didn't have an ounce to spare. I knew that it was vital to stay in the present moment with no regrets, fears, or worries. As I slowly gained control over my thoughts, I enjoyed the beautiful walk past St. Paul's Chapel toward the World Trade Center. All the way home, I marveled at the simple elegance of everything around me. By the time I arrived home, it was only 12 hours before takeoff. The future would come to me no matter what I did, so why think about it in advance?

Once home, I sat down in the chair closest to the door. Yes, there was exhaustion, but I felt anticipation and excitement as well. I have had this same feeling on many a Christmas Eve. All was in order and everything around me was silent and still. There was no more rushing around; the presents were wrapped and placed under the tree. I was pleased, cheerful, and content with all the preparations that had been made for the big day. Then it hit me. There was one last-minute thing that I had totally forgotten about, one last gift that I needed to find and wrap up before I could settle down for my long winter's nap. What to do about Facebook?

To Post and What to Post?

Now, many of you may think that this sounds trivial or shallow, but it is not. I am quite a presence on this particular social media. I keep in touch with past students, opera singers, former college friends, and the like. I always send birthday greetings, congratulations for big events, condolences, and support to many people. They would all eventually hear the news about my condition, but if I simply left without a word it would be devastating for some of them. I wanted to leave behind something that would let them know that I was thinking about them and had not just abandoned them. I also wanted something that would become a fond remembrance of me in the event that I passed away; yet, I had to do it in such a way as to not raise alarm or concern. I promised the Playhouse that I would not make my diagnosis public until an announcement had been officially made to the student body; therefore, I needed to be very crafty and clever in order to accommodate everything without arousing suspicion. Inspiration struck in the form of a wonderful post that would throw everyone off the track. It would bring comfort in my absence after the news broke but would not reveal too much information. For those who knew me more intimately, however, they could read between the lines and know that something was amiss and do further investigation on their own.

The post read as follows:

"My Dear ALL! I will not be on Facebook for a bit! I am going on a very fabulous and exotic journey! I will be without the ability to communicate: SO PLEASE, do not think I am ignoring you. For all of you that will be having birthdays, I am wishing you the happiest! Those of you with glorious life events, I am wishing you congrats and blessings. Those of you with loss or pain or sorrow, I offer you my profound condolences, strength, and courage. Those of you who are having fun, DO IT WITH ALL THE GUSTO you are able, and for those of you who feel alone, remember, you are never alone. Those of you who are afraid, there is nothing to fear. And those of you who are content, you are the master of your soul, so go forward and have a blessed and fruitful life. Love and blessings to you all until I return! BIG HUG! Gary"

Wrapping up this final gift had a wonderful and cathartic affect on my state of mind. In a strange way, it now truly was Christmas. I was filled with the spirit of joy and goodwill toward all. I could go to bed happy and content that I had done the very best I could do for those who have known and loved me. This post would be something of a comfort and a reminder not to be sad, fearful, or worried for me, but to keep on living their lives fully. That is exactly what I wanted for all of them, even in the event of my death. Everything that I had written, I would send off in the morning before I left the house and could now go to bed and get some good sleep.

Haunted by My Own Ghost

Exhaustion was beginning to take hold, and just as I was finishing up on the computer, I caught a glimpse of myself in the mirror. I appeared so horribly thin and gaunt that I actually looked like the ghost of Jacob Marley. Whether it was the sheer exhaustion or I was just a little too high from all of the Christmas cheer, I laughed hysterically at this parallel with poor Jacob. Then, a thought shot through me that perhaps I would not even wake up in the morning. Maybe this was as far as I was going to go and unlike Scrooge would not get another chance at life. This thought did not depress me, nor did I banish it from my mind. I was instead compelled to reflect on it.

After a short while, I sensed that I should go back over the post that I had just written. I reread the line, "And for those of you who are content, you are the master of your soul, so go forward..." What a wonderful line, and it was true. My own words offered themselves back to me as comfort and solace. Indeed, I felt completely content even if my journey stopped at this very second, and I truly did feel as though I was the master of my soul. I had played this round exactly the way I wanted to play it. I had no regrets and no feelings of bitterness about any of this. Lastly and most importantly, I would continue to move forward no matter what. Though I should "walk through the valley of the shadow of death," there would be no turning back, and I would do it with "all the gusto" that I could muster up.

Chapter 6 – Here We Go

If you could kick the person in the pants responsible for most of your
trouble, you wouldn't sit for a month.

Theodore Roosevelt

A Christmas Hangover

The following morning, I woke up in advance of the alarm. I had slept quite well and was still feeling some of the Christmas cheer from the night before. Except instead of awakening as a robust and renewed Scrooge, I continued to resemble the tortured agony of a Jacob Marley. (Oh well, so much for Christmas miracles.) The past week, filled with its difficult challenges, combined with the weight and blood loss had taken its toll. Thank goodness, I was only hours away from some kind of relief. I had managed to wrap up my life in only five short days, and I was ready to walk out the door with no regrets. I knew that once I was immersed in the peace and solitude of my fantasy island clinic, I would only have myself to take care of and nothing else.

I had concluded that, in every respect, illness is a work overload for the afflicted person. In addition to the disease and all of its complications, exhaustive amounts of energy are expended on taking care of others, dealing with doctors, and making decisions. I found that this is more physically, mentally, and emotionally debilitating than the disease itself; then there is the fear factor. Had I been terrified of my death sentence this entire time, I am certain that an aneurysm would have erupted like Mount Vesuvius. I wondered how many people have had a similar experience to mine. I would presume many, and all of this, coupled with my non-traditional bent, made getting out of Dodge even sweeter.

Preparing to Exit

I was glad that I woke up much earlier than needed because I would have ample time to meditate. I had been meditating on a regular basis for quite awhile and always found it very soothing and calming; now under the current circumstances it was mandatory. It also afforded me a bit of time to bask in the energy of my home. I love my apartment because it has an old-world feel to it. The building was built in the 1920s, which is one of my favorite eras, and it has an incredible energy. My apartment is filled with meaningful pieces that I have collected over the years. Each piece is symbolic of someone who was very special to me in my life, many of whom are no longer living on the planet. Their memories and my love for them are well represented in their former possessions. I believe that all things are alive and filled with the energy of the universe, so I was determined to leave everything with a solemn and proper farewell. This was possibly one of the last times I might have ever been here again, and the actor in me refused to make a bad exit, especially if this turned out to be a final one.

Once my meditation was complete, I packed rather quickly. Since the hospital provides all clothing and toiletries to its guests, there wasn't much to take. I packed an extra set of clothes, a few personal items, and the score to Rigoletto, my favorite opera of all time. This title role is one that I had always wanted to sing but never did. I so love the music that it felt comforting to have the score and the recordings of my coaching sessions on the role with me. Besides, if things turned out badly, I was going to request that I be cremated with the score and make Rigoletto mine for eternity.

The Final Curtain

The moment of truth arrived, and just as I closed the door to my apartment, a fear came over me. It felt as though I would not be returning. I quickly caught the anxiety underneath this thought, and instead of stuffing it or ignoring it, I completely embraced and welcomed it. Within a few minutes, the fear slowly dissipated. I actually smiled at what my mind was doing to me in that moment. I knew that the most powerful position I could maintain throughout the rest of this journey was to remain calm and true to my heart. I marveled at the vigilance necessary to accomplish this. Fear seemed to await me at every corner and was ready to take me down. I needed to stand vigilant at the door of my heart to prevent him from entering—if only I had realized that this was a precursor of things to come that day. Innocently, I closed my door and locked it. I was resolved to leave fear behind, and like Nora in "A Doll's House," there would be no turning back.

I descended down the stairs to Mary's apartment. I was leaving her in charge of everything while I was away. We have known each other for the past 25 years, and I trusted her implicitly. As she opened the door, I could see the anxiety in her face. It was apparent that she had not slept much. She is a courageous soul and gave me a big warm welcome as I entered her apartment. We discussed details about everything that she needed to take care of while I was away. I also had a list of things I wanted her to help my sister with in the event of my death. She listened very carefully and made detailed notes. After I was done, she looked at me very intently and stated that if I did not come back alive she was going to kill me. I howled with laughter. A text arrived that the car was downstairs waiting for me. I handed her my mail key and grandly pronounced,

"Your Majesty, His Highness must now bid you adieu. I leave my entire kingdom in your most worthy hands!"

She rolled her eyes replying, "I will take great royal care of everything. Now get the hell out of here before you wake the rest of the kingdom!" I exited, feeling extremely proud of myself as I walked down the stairs. I left exactly the way I had intended: No drama, no tears or anxiety, only laughter and tenderness.

On the Road Less Traveled

The driver may have suspected that something was not quite right when I appeared through the door because he immediately ran up to take my bag. Perhaps he also saw the ghost of Jacob Marley. It was an exquisite morning. The sun had just begun to rise, and the air was still a bit cool and breezy. As we drove, the driver questioned me about my trip. I told him that I was going to a spa in Mexico for a much-needed vacation. The words just flew out of my mouth. I smiled because it DID feel as though I was going on a vacation—a complete vacation package with no strings attached and not even a return ticket.

I began to feel a sense of elation that was similar to what I had experienced shortly after the diagnosis. For the first time, I realized what a truly amazing adventure I was on and how blessed I was to be making this journey. I arrived at the airport in record time and flew through security. The flight was on time, and I was able to board early. Things couldn't have gone more smoothly if I'd planned them myself. Once in my seat, I had an immense sense of relief. I felt as though I had just finished running a marathon. There was nothing more to do. I had done everything that I could, and as Lady Macbeth says to her hubby, "What is done cannot be undone."

A Bump in the Air

The flight was rather empty, and I had an entire row of seats to stretch out in. The cabin pressure had a bigger affect on me than usual, and I quickly fell into a rather tranquil sleep. Suddenly, out of nowhere, we ran into some unexpected turbulence. A sudden and extreme dip in the plane occurred, and I could have sworn I felt something happen in my lower torso. Immediately, my mind jumped to the tumor cracking apart. For the first time since all of this began, I felt a sense of panic. Extreme panic.

What to do? Call the steward over and say, "Excuse me, would you happen to have something for a dead man?" Should I even mention it and risk panicking the others? I forgot about these questions and immediately began to calm myself down. I told myself that the worst that would happen is my body would not be discovered until landing. I convinced myself there was nothing else to be done. If it indeed happened, it would be painlessly over in 10 minutes or at least that is what the doctor told me. I looked at my watch and began the countdown. I laughed to myself and thought, "Two takeoffs in one day, and I didn't even have to change planes."

I broke out in a cold sweat and felt my heart racing. I worked on my Alexander directions and took slow, deep breaths. I was grateful for the last 16 years I'd devoted to the technique and for the ability to regain my center so that I would not die in a panic nor cause one. I would go out as gracefully as possible, and I could not be closer to heaven if I tried. After a few minutes, nothing happened except that both the plane and I began to calm down. I continued to breathe deeply as my heart rate returned to normal. I checked my watch again, and it was past the 10-minute mark. I had made it, and although shaken, I was totally fine.

The impact of this surprise punch had nearly taken me down for the count. In this particular instance, fear was the bigger culprit. I thought, "Holy cow. My thoughts are as deadly as my condition." I made a pact with myself that I would not let this happen again. I would take great care not to jump to any more conclusions and instead remain calm and cool in the interim. I had already been through so much up to this point. Why allow one crazy moment to spoil it all? I was grateful for this experience and much wiser for the wear.

We landed without further incident, and I headed toward the appropriate exit where the driver was to pick me up. I grabbed a veggie sandwich and a bottle of water before going to my designated spot. Little did I know that this would be the last bread that would pass through my lips for a very long time to come. I was just finishing lunch when my driver arrived, and we went into the van for a ride over the Mexican border. There was a BPA-free bottle with my name written on it. It was filled with the water they purify and mineralize at the facility. I had a sip and could sense an odd difference in the water from what I had just purchased at the airport. I rarely taste any difference in waters unless it is well water. Luckily, it tasted good because it was the only water available to drink while I was there.

Entering Paradise

We easily crossed the border, and I took in the views of the Baja shoreline. They were breathtaking. I wondered how a medical facility could exist in the midst of this paradise? The air, the atmosphere, the energy, and every other aspect of the environment felt as though it was penetrating my cells. From the moment I stepped out of the van, I did not feel as though there was anything wrong with me but rather that everything was right with me. It really WAS a vacation on a fantasy island. How anything of medical importance could possibly take place here was beyond my comprehension.

There to greet me was a lovely young woman whose name was the same as my neighbor, Mary. I took this to be a good omen. She knew my name and pretty much everything about me. She wanted me to come with her to what she referred to as the "mansion" to sign all the necessary papers. After the paperwork was complete, she took me on a short tour of the facility. It was absolutely gorgeous and very regal looking. She always referred to the residents at the institute as guests, never patients. There were massage rooms, salons, dining rooms, pools, and gardens but nothing of a medical nature. I mentioned to her that I would be having surgery here and was hoping to see where that was done. She stated that I would have to talk to my doctor about that. As we continued, I became a bit uneasy about her answer and the lack of medical rooms and equipment.

She brought me to my glorious room. It was gorgeous and huge with a magnificent view of the ocean. There was an adjoining companion room prepared for the arrival of my sister who would be there in time for my surgery. My wardrobe was hung neatly in the closet. It consisted of workout pants, t-shirts, shorts, zipper-down jackets, and a bright white robe. All clothing was made of organic cotton and was pretty much cream colored or white. She told me to change and be ready to attend lunch in the dining room within the hour. She instructed me to call the front desk if I had any questions and to make myself at home.

Paradise Lost

Make myself at home? How do you do that in heaven? My mind was becoming uneasy. Why did I not see one thing that even remotely suggested a medical facility? Not even a first aid kit. This was a high-end spa, not a clinic and certainly not a hospital. For the first time, I felt unnerved about my decision to come to Mexico for treatment. I sensed another wave of panic quickly brewing within me; however, I learned my lesson from the plane and was resolved not to play out another fear-based drama, so I decided to call my sister.

Her voice of reason broke through all of my ill doubts. She reminded me that this was not the ordinary method for dealing with cancer; therefore, how on earth could I expect this facility to be ordinary? She reminded me that this was the basic reason I'd chosen to leave the country in the first place. I confessed that, thus far, everything was exactly the way it had been stated on the website and what I'd been told over the phone. Also, this was a Sunday, and I was told that not much would be going on. By the time we ended our conversation, I was much calmer and assured her that I would not jump off of my gorgeous balcony. She laughed and said I'd better not because she was excited to see the place for herself, and suicide would really mess things up. She was certainly correct about that, and we laughed over the entire thing.

After we hung up, I realized that I was really perturbed with myself over these drama-filled reactions. Why was I having these all of a sudden? I hadn't had these kinds of episodes at home after my diagnosis, but now, on the very day I arrive, I had two in a row. I was especially annoyed with myself since I had been truly at peace with all my decisions and actions. Why was I now so jumpy and reactive? I would have to save this debate for another time, however, because I needed to get ready for action. I was becoming desperate for food, and so I changed into my appropriate garb. I joked with myself that I would go as "undercover guest 007" to find out exactly where the secret medical rooms were hidden. Feeling better and more jovial, I marched out the door ready for my mission.

Devine Dining and Beyond

I arrived at the main dining room promptly for lunch. Later, I found out that all the guests who were undergoing treatments always dined in this particular room. It had a spectacular view of the immaculately kept grounds and of the ocean. Some people were already sitting at a large table, and I asked if I could join them. I was happy that they accepted my request because they looked like they knew their way around the place. Conversation was challenging, however, because how do you begin? "So, what are you in for?" would not exactly be the best opening line. Fortunately, the arrival of the food was far more captivating than any conversation. It was without a doubt one of the most wonderful organic meals I had ever eaten. It was so good that it seemed as though it couldn't possibly be healthy. The presentation alone made it appear sinful. The hospital believes that food is considered medicine and was part of the therapy. My table companions had nothing but rave reviews about the facility and of course the food. I did not ask too many questions and listened to whatever information they were comfortable divulging on their own. Their critiques buoyed me immensely as did the cuisine.

After numerous refills of my plate, I finally had my fill. For well over a week, I had not been this satisfied after a meal. I was sure that I would be gaining more weight in no time if I continued to eat in this way. I went for a walk around the grounds and discovered a wonderful place that would become one of my favorite spots. It was a very private terrace that was perched directly above the ocean. The water crashed on the rocks below, and it made me feel as though I was floating above the ocean. I loved this place, and as the weeks progressed, it became one of my treasured meditation spots.

The First Awakening

In the center of the grounds, there was a very large and hilly lawn that is used for grounding therapy. It was recommended that the guests could either lie down in or walk barefoot through the grass. This also became another of my cherished pastimes, and I would often do it with my eyes closed for a richer meditative experience. In time, I learned to treat everything that I did as a meditation. Whatever treatment, therapy, or moment I was involved with, would become just another living, breathing meditative opportunity.

While slowly walking through the grass, I realized what my recent fearful reactions were about. I felt guilty over having left everyone behind and was punishing myself for it. The caretaking champion within me was still struggling over the pain of disappointing others. Since my childhood, every time I failed to make others happy, I could not bear the repercussions. My youthful perspective believed that I was the main cause for all of the misery that ensued and carried the burden of guilt through the aftermath. Wouldn't you know that my guilt would be alive and well here in Mexico? I clearly saw how my intense responses over the incident on the plane and the lack of medical equipment were seen as failures in my eyes. These two failures provided me with enough ammunition to wage an attack on myself for the wake of disappointment and unhappiness I had left behind. Despite the fact that I believed wholeheartedly in my decision, my guilty conscience demanded vengeance for having made my quick escape.

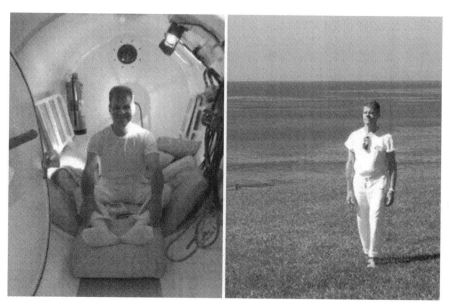

PHOTO 4: Hyperbaric chamber & Overhang by the Water (Paradise Island)

The Old Rugged Cross

What an insidious and deadly habit to have hanging around my neck, especially in light of my current circumstances. I wondered how many people in dire straights have experienced this same guilt. I was saddened by the number of times I unwittingly accepted my role as the guilty victim. What good was it for me or anyone else to walk around with this heavy burden? What did it matter whether I made others unhappy or dissatisfied with my actions? I decided that I was not going to allow these burdensome guilty feelings run me around anymore. All of this was happening to me, not to anyone else, and I was taking full responsibility for whatever may come my way. It crossed my mind that perhaps this was why I had become so seriously ill in the first place. Could this cancer be my ultimate revenge and punishment upon myself for my past failures? No one will ever know, nor does it matter. Whatever the cause, I was finished punishing myself for it and refused to nail myself to a cross any longer. I vowed to be freed from all of this, and if nothing else, I would die completely in peace.

I lay down on the grass and felt as though a great weight had been lifted. I looked up at the magnificent sky while the day's events raced through my mind and heart. It was as though the very energy of the environment was already magically casting a spell over me. I was amazed how nothing else seemed to matter other than this present moment. I no longer minded anything that had occurred in my life and was even calm about what might occur. The past, present, and future all seemed to melt away with nothing but peace surrounding me. I now completely understood that all I ever really needed to do was to simply let go of the meanderings of my ego mind and leave my past and future alone. The title of Eckhart Tolle's "The Power of Now" echoed through me. I felt as though the parts of me that were no longer helpful flew away while the helpful ones remained. Here I was on the first day of my fantasy island experience practically transported into a sense of ease and wholeness. I could not even begin to imagine what the week would bring.

Chapter 7 – Reacquainting with my Legacy

Nothing splendid has ever been achieved except by those who dared believe that something inside of them was superior to circumstance.

- Bruce Fairchild Barton

Schedule of Synchronicities

The following morning, I was awakened by music coming from the television set. They automatically go on as your wake-up call at the facility. I had received my schedule the night before and learned where all the hidden medical rooms were. My day was booked solid, so I got up and got ready rather quickly. I first reported to the lab where samples of my blood were taken, and then it was off to the nurse's station. There I would be weighed, have all of my vitals checked, and receive my daily medicines. To my surprise, in fewer than 24 hours, I dropped another pound despite the fact that I was allowed to stuff myself like a pig. I was assured not to worry about this and that weight loss while on the pure organic diet was exactly what the doctors wanted to have happen; it indicated that the tumor had to work harder for nourishment.

Then I was off to a meditation class that I totally loved and adored. It was led by a man whom I did not know at all, but his clothing color indicated that he was a doctor. The clothing color was the key method to determine the Who's Who game throughout the facility. He emanated kindness and compassion, and I anticipated that he would lead a wonderful class. He did exactly that and began by making it clear that there were no rules to follow. He encouraged everyone to follow their intuition and sit, lie, or be in whatever position was comfortable for them. This would be a theme throughout the duration of my stay. No one was ever subjected to many rules or regulations except for two: 1. Never leave the premises without permission. 2. Never socialize with other guests who were not interested.

After meditation, I went to breakfast. Once again, the hunger was astounding to me. It was a gnawing, harsh feeling that seemed to be steadily growing stronger. If making the tumor angry was what they wanted, they were doing a spectacular job. Rosemary's baby was becoming extremely agitated with me even though I was easily ingesting twice my normal amount of food. I could not even imagine how our relationship was going to end. After devouring my lion's share of breakfast, I was now ready to begin my busy schedule. Seven doctors were assigned to my team. Dr. M., who had interviewed me over the phone, was in charge of my entire case, and I would meet the rest of them within the next couple of days.

Every day, I had appointments with various practitioners and therapists who the team believed would be the most advantageous for my progress. I was off to my first session with the psychologist for an evaluation. Dr. M. mentioned in our phone interview that they were interested in my mental/emotional condition, and since this was my first appointment, I guessed that they were not kidding. I was assigned to a Dr. J. who, to my utter surprise, was the very same doctor who had led the meditation. I couldn't have been happier, and he could not have been a better choice. I took this as another sign that the universe was truly working its magic specifically with me in mind.

The conversation got off to a great start, and I mentioned how much I had enjoyed his class. I told him everything that had been going on with me and described the odd and inexplicable sense of peace that had been following me around. I added that there were only the two brief lapses when I left home yesterday and explained why I felt they had occurred. I also talked about the irony of feeling so uplifted while something so deadly was growing inside of me. I related my beliefs surrounding the miraculous and the inexplicable. I used the example of how I was assigned to him for this session and told him about finding Anita Moorjani's story long before my own crisis arose.

Another Awakening on the Way

He changed the topic of the conversation and asked me about my earliest experience with death. My paternal grandmother was at the top of that list. She died when I was only seven years old and was my first and most profound experience. She was an extraordinary being whose sheer energy seemed to transform a room, and I simply adored her. She came onto this earth bestowed with many amazing gifts but above them all were her psychic abilities. These allowed her to sustain a living for her family during the depression. I was fascinated by her inexplicable powers and as a child vowed to possess them, ergo, my current fascination with heightened sensibilities and the miraculous. After her death, my father slipped into a deep depression. His over-drinking escalated into full-blown alcoholism. Money became scarce and chaos abundant. I believe it surprised everyone how key my grandmother had been to our lives. Although my father loathed her vehemently while she was alive, he fell completely apart with her death.

The more I spoke about her, the more akin I felt to her. I now identified with her in ways that I had never thought possible. During her illness, she had gotten little comfort or support from my father or any of her other children. I had not received much of that either. My greatest support came from my sister while my grandmother's biggest supporter was her daughter-in-law, my mother. Talking about her struggle and isolation produced a profound wave of grief that washed over me. I began to weep uncontrollably. It was as though I was experiencing both of our lives simultaneously. I cannot really explain this clearly because it made no sense at the time nor afterwards.

I was not necessarily upset for her or for myself as individuals per se, but somehow, I was mourning a greater tragedy of sorts. Why did anyone ever have to go through this deadly dance? Then a poignant memory popped into my head out of nowhere as I wept. It was the last time I ever saw my grandmother alive.

The Remembered Kiss

I was waiting in the hospital parking lot with my twin brother, George, and my oldest brother, Mark. Children were not allowed to visit, so my grandmother requested that the three of us would stand outside her hospital window at a designated time. We all waited in the family car for what seemed to be an eternity when my older brother finally herded us out of the car and made us stand in a specific place. High above us, one of the windows flew open and framed within it was my grandmother waving her long arms in our direction. I began waving back to her like a madman. I had not had a glimpse of her for quite some time, and I was beyond exuberant. She then put her hand up to her mouth to blow us a kiss. I remember seeing something fall from her hand and slowly descend toward us. At first, I thought it was a feather or a ribbon because it seemed to gently float on the air, but then it simply disappeared. Shortly after that, something touched the top of my head and it felt like a kiss. I could not believe it. A strange tingling sensation went through my entire body. I was in total elation and was sure that the kiss was meant only for me. I asked my brothers what that thing was that she blew down to us, and they looked at me like I was crazy. I told them that I felt something hit the top of my head but in their typically curt manner, they told me it must have been bird shit.

PHOTO 5: RAMSEY FAMILY (TOP, LEFT TO RIGHT): MARK, MOTHER DOLORES, GARY, PAULA, DAD MARK, GEORGE; (BOTTOM LEFT) GRANDMOTHER; (BOTTOM RIGHT): GARY & TWIN BROTHER GEORGE, 6 YEARS OLD

I knew with certainty they had to be wrong. I had long been used to my grandmother's mystical and magical ways and had witnessed her psychic abilities firsthand many times. This event, however, surpassed all the rest. Could it have been a child's overactive imagination or the inaccuracy of a child's memory? Absolutely, I would not even bother to argue the point; however, my perceptual reality told me that my grandmother had kissed me on the top of my head, and as ridiculous as it may sound,

I still concur with this phenomenon today. From my perspective, no matter how extraordinary or unreal anything may appear to be, it is the total truth for the one who has experienced it. Perhaps it exists only in their personal, virtual reality, but isn't that where everything exists for all of us anyway? Isn't reality simply our interpretation of what we experience or think we experience via the brain/mind?

Death's Power Revisited

This session brought back not only the pain of my grandmother's death but the misery that followed. Things were never the same again for my entire family. Shortly before her funeral, my father became completely unhinged by her loss, and his personality, drinking, and temper went wildly off the rails. I was an eyewitness to how powerful death could be and became enamored of its potency. I remembered how my young mind's fascination stripped away any fear of it and instead, produced a deep longing to die. I prayed for death to come and take me out of the isolation to which I had been abandoned. Death came to represent everlasting salvation, and my final kiss sealed the deal for me. Fortunately, this desire wore away with time and had been all but lost until today. After I recounted all of these old memories to the doctor, it was unremarkable that I did not fear death. What was remarkable to me, however, was that I now saw my grandmother's death in a whole new light. It no longer struck me as the nightmarish tragedy that I had survived, but I was now filled with gratitude for having lived and experienced it.

Once again, as on the lawn the day before, I felt lighter and freer due to this realization. My entire concept of my past and my participation in it were recreated before my very eyes. How was all of this possible in simply one session of therapy and one aha moment on the lawn by myself? I had been through countless therapy sessions in my life and had never gotten these results. I could only attribute this success to the fact that the stakes were high, and there was no time to waste. It was as though my mind and soul were ready and willing to acknowledge the imperfections of the past and realize their perfection. Already these two realizations brought more relief to me than I had felt in decades. It was as though I had been healed right then and there. The cancer seemed almost irrelevant in certain respects because I felt so vibrantly alive. It was as though every cell of my being was strengthened to deal with what lay ahead and immense support was pouring into me from all corners of the universe.

A New Lease

I was joyously propelled into the days that followed. The doctors assessed everything about my health and worked to promote the perfect conditions for the removal of my tumor. Each day, I felt as though I was in the healing zone because every treatment seemed to improve my overall well-being and health. It all was unfolding so perfectly, in fact, that death was no longer even in the picture. It became nothing more than an old friend who would eventually stop by to pick me up when the time was right. I knew that I would be going with him one day anyway, so why be worried or concerned? The concept of dying became as joyous as the life I was now living. They seemed inseparable. Sometimes it was hard to believe that there was anything wrong with me.

This joyous state of being did not go unnoticed by the rest of my team. One day while having a spa treatment, one of the attendants remarked that she was sure I would be totally healed. I asked her how she knew this.

"Because every guest with an attitude like yours is always cured."

It made perfect sense to me. Her prophecy, however, did not change a thing. I continued to live in the wonderful paradox between life and death without any wish for a specific outcome. In the Alexander world, we use the term "end gaining," which means to keep one's mind and actions focused on a desired final result. This is an inefficient use of our energy, and the student is encouraged to let go of this habit. I now was practicing the art of living with no end result in sight whatsoever and was slowly beginning to master it. I lived fully in this sacred space as much as possible and grew to love it more and more with each passing day.

My current preoperative program consisted of a wide variety of therapies: reiki, reflexology, exercising in heated pools, infrared sauna, long hours in the hyperbaric chamber, and the quiet room. The quiet room is very difficult to explain other than it is like stepping into heaven. It has full views of the ocean, and it contains cutting-edge electronic equipment designed to stimulate the body's own natural healing ability. The only thing I can tell you about these treatments is that they were out of this world. The results and progress reports from my total medical regiment were continuously entered into a computerized chart. Everyone knew instantly what was going on with me from the moment I entered any of the treatment rooms. If I even mentioned at the front desk that I had not slept well, it became public knowledge. There were no secrets in Shangri La.

During a meeting with my surgeon, he agreed with my medical team that it would be best to continue my pre-op treatments and postpone the surgery. Everyone was pleased with all of the results thus far and felt it wise to continue. Their philosophy of "the treatments prior to surgery determine the success of the surgery" was working well. All of this was in stark contrast to my first diagnosis that insisted surgery should be done immediately and that "yesterday would have been the best day." Though I had no idea which medical approach was correct or would work, it did not matter to me. I was having a gloriously incredible time.

In fact, things were progressing so well, the doctors wanted another CAT scan. To do this, I would have to be taken off the premises and driven to another facility for the actual scan. A car was arranged for the following morning. The problem was I would not be able to eat for at least 10 hours prior to the scan. This was unbearable for me to even think about. I could barely make seven hours without eating food, and that was ONLY if I was asleep and not using up any energy. I had no idea how I would make it through the following day. The team realized how difficult this would be for me but explained that a new scan was vital. I was comforted by the fact that I would be accompanied by one of my favorite staff members, Rene, who would immediately give me a special meal prepared by the kitchen once the scan was complete.

Do Dreams Really Come True?

I went to bed earlier than usual thinking that the longer I slept, the less hungry I would be. I fell into a very deep sleep and had one of the most remarkable dreams I have possibly ever had. My grandmother appeared to me in my room. This certainly was of no surprise–during the dream and after waking–due to her appearance in my therapy session a few days earlier. She was dressed in white and emanating an angelic quality throughout the room. Her appearance was reminiscent of the Ghost of Christmas Past visiting Ebenezer Scrooge. Clearly, the theme from my Christmas revelry on the eve of my departure was being continued. She entered through the balcony doors and looked like a younger and more regal version of herself. When I saw her, I was amazed that she found me here in Mexico and asked her how she did that. She smiled and told me to come with her. She led me off the balcony, and we flew over the water to some faraway place.

There, my father and his sister, Barbara, awaited us. Both of them appeared younger and more vibrant than I remember either of them during my lifetime. They were extremely happy and excited to see me and were celebrating my upcoming event. I tried to find out exactly what event they were referring to, but to no avail. They seemed to be preparing me for something and giving me things to hold onto as they draped things over me. All the while, they continued to celebrate and dance around me. In the dream, I could not imagine why they were doing this or what it meant. One thing was quite clear, however, they were united in their task.

When I awoke, I remembered most of the dream and was extremely perplexed for a variety of reasons. First and foremost, I have not dreamed about any of them in many years and certainly never together. During my childhood, I rarely even saw them together in the same room at the same time. When it did happen, it always ended badly. Secondly, during their lifetimes, they all shared a rather negative and bleak view of the world. So, for all of them to be joyously celebratory was highly uncharacteristic, to say the least. My grandmother was the non-drinker and the more reserved member of the trio while my father and his sister were completely the opposite. Their alcohol consumption was epic, and both of them tended toward boisterous and argumentative behavior. The happiest of occasions were marred by dark, foreboding clouds; therefore, seeing them together in this jubilant state was my only glimpse at what could have been but never came to pass. It nearly brought tears to my eyes.

The Long Day's Journey

I quickly wrote everything down about the dream before I forgot it. When I was done, I prepared for my challenging CAT scan assignment. I decided to wear the outfit I had worn when I arrived in Mexico instead of my new wardrobe. While dressing, I noticed a huge difference in how the clothing fit me. I had only lost about three more pounds since my arrival, but the difference was immense. I was at the point where every ounce was of vital importance. As I adjusted my belt in the mirror to keep my pants safely in place, the dream instantly popped in my head. Was it somehow preparing me for a bigger and more permanent journey? I tossed it off but did admit to myself that if death were in the cards, then I would play those cards to the best of my ability until the end of the game. I was not going to leave the planet a loser and certainly not a sore one. I reminded myself how happy I was in my decision to come to Mexico and that no matter what the outcome, my last moments were going to be fantastic ones.

I hurried down to reception and was met by Rene. I always enjoyed having him around because he had a great energy and was always very helpful. We were accompanied by another man whose name was Dennis. He was a friend of the creator and head of the facility and was having a medical test done as well. He was a very kind person and had led a fascinating life. He mentioned that he was a friend of Dr. Wayne Dyer whom I admired and had read many of his books. In fact, it was Dr. Dyer's first radio interview with Anita Moorjani that had originally brought her to my attention.

Dennis was a great conversationalist, and we talked about a multitude of things that kept me thoroughly entertained during the ride. This was very fortunate because within an hour, my hunger was becoming immense, and the conversation helped to steady me. I was doing my best to remain calm, but by the time we arrived at the testing facility, my body was visibly shaking. It felt as though the tumor was about to devour me from the inside out. This was the first time I was unable to eat when the baby demanded it, and I have never experienced this sort of ravenous hunger ever before. It made my heart weep for those who die of starvation.

Luckily, they took me right away, and as soon as I was finished, Rene was holding my lunch with a big smile on his face. I did my very best not to tear into it like a lion that had just made a kill. Once I began to eat, calmness descended upon me, and I enjoyed a delightful ride back. I made it just in time for lunch and could not have been happier.

I quickly changed clothes and continued my heavy appointment load. I no longer had much time to think about the dream and thought it best to just forget about it. I had lots to do because of my sister's arrival the following day. I had prepared her as best I could for what to expect and especially how I looked. I was a whopping 182 pounds when she saw me on the previous Memorial Day, and now I was desperately clinging to 140 pounds, a weight I have not been since my adolescence.

Sister, Support, and Symbolism

The following day, Paula arrived in ample time for lunch. She fell in love with the place at first sight. I introduced her to all of my new acquaintances, and she even accompanied me to my next appointment with the doctor. She was very impressed with the efficiency and kindness of the entire staff. During the meeting with Dr. M., he reported how happy he was with the results of the scan and had already forwarded them to the surgeon. It was becoming clear that surgery would be in a few days on Tuesday, September 8th, and that it would have to be done at the hospital in Tijuana. They needed a larger team and more equipment, so it was easier to move me there rather than bringing everything to me. I told Paula all about my meeting with the surgeon and mentioned how he had ironically spent three years at Sloan Kettering in a special surgical program. I thought this was an amazing coincidence that I should travel all the way to Mexico only to end up with a surgeon trained at Sloan where I was first recommended to go.

The next couple of days were excellent ones for us both. Paula shadowed me as I went to my appointments even though I encouraged her to take advantage of some of the spa treatments. She insisted that she was fine and was kept busy enough without adding spa appointments. Between dealing with her daughter, Jade, who was beginning the school year at a brand new one and her own affairs, she had plenty on her plate. Plus, she was fast becoming my full-time secretary as well. This was mainly because my personal cell phone had unfortunately died and went to phone heaven with all of my contacts. Whoever did not have Paula's number was unable to reach me nor could I call them unless I was able to recall their number from memory. It was just as well because I was told to restrict my exposure to electromagnetic equipment. The facility did not feel it was healthy for someone like myself to electronically indulge. Paula did not mind the extra workload and was a great help to me. I enjoyed and appreciated having her love and support as we neared the operation date.

A Reoccurrence

All was going quite well until two nights before my surgery. Wouldn't you know that I had the exact same dream about my grandmother, father, and aunt. Only this time, it was more vivid and a bit more disconcerting because it truly felt as though they were preparing me for my impending arrival on the other side. Death seemed to definitely be on my dance card, and although I was not frightened by the possibility, I thought it unwise to ignore the premonition any longer. I decided to tell my sister about both of the dreams and disclose my feelings about this most recent one.

She listened in utter rapture. She was as surprised and shocked by them as I was. We were in full agreement that there was a larger symbolic meaning going on behind them. Beyond the obvious family connection, the contrasts with regards to their demeanor and personalities were (as my sister stated) unsettling to say the least. I also recounted everything that happened in the therapy session before the first dream occurred. It was clear that my subconscious wanted to tell me something, but what was it? After unloading this truckload of information, Paula remarked that there was only one thing about the dreams that struck her as ominous and truly frightened her. I asked her what that was. She replied, "that they were all getting along with each other."

We howled with laughter. It truly cut the severity of the entire matter. Upon further contemplation, we realized their congeniality WAS pretty scary but continued to laugh over it. Once we regained ourselves, I confessed to her that no matter what, I had no regrets concerning my decision to come here. She felt the exact same way about her decision to come and support me. The dream never occurred again.

An Unforeseen Blessing

The following day, Paula received a call from my colleague Anne at the Neighborhood Playhouse. She asked how things were going, and Paula told her that I was available to speak. Once we were on the phone together, Anne wanted to know if I remembered Debbra Gill whom she had mentioned before I left town. I said that I did. She told me that she also works with people psychically during surgery. Anne wanted my permission for Debbra to work on me and to arrange a prayer circle during my surgery. I was so touched by the kindness of the gesture that I quickly agreed to it. After all, it would do no harm whatsoever, and I could use all the help I could get. She needed the date and the exact location of the surgery, both of which I knew. She also needed to know the exact time that it would be performed, but I told her she would have to be in touch with Paula to coordinate that detail.

Afterwards, when I discussed it with Paula, she agreed it was only a help and not a hindrance.

"Besides," Paula jokingly replied, "maybe it will put a damper on the welcoming party Grandma Ramsey is throwing for you!"

Very funny, but also, absolutely correct—the surgery was tricky and certain variables were still unknown, so I was more than grateful to have the extra energy surrounding me during this ordeal. Once again, the universe was watching out for me, and things were falling effortlessly into place.

Chapter 8 – Hark the Herald Angels Come

There are only two ways to live your life. One is as though nothing is a miracle. The other is as though everything is a miracle.

— *Albert Einstein*

D-Day Approaches

On Monday, September 7th, we departed for the hospital shortly after lunch and bid a fond farewell to the medical staff and the other guests. We were taken by car to Tijuana and met by a staff member who had left ahead of us. He was in charge of all the arrangements and details at the hospital. After I signed the final papers, we went up to my suite. I use the term suite because it was simply exquisite. It was equipped with every comfort and convenience imaginable. Paula and I even had our own private bathrooms. The nursing staff was absolutely terrific, the service incredible, and the only drawback was that almost everyone spoke Spanish exclusively. Luckily, I remembered enough Spanish from a foreign exchange program to Chile that I was awarded in high school. I lived there for several months while attending school and spoke primarily in Spanish. Paula unfortunately was dependent upon me for all communication. Only the surgeon spoke English but, he would be with me. She would be totally stranded during my surgery, and when she realized the gravity of her situation, she looked at me with great intent and said, "You'd better not die."

I simply responded, "I'll see what I can do."

Shortly after we arrived in the room, the surgeon called and said that there was a slight hitch with my red blood cell count. It was too weak for surgery and he was ordering a blood transfusion. This did not come as much of a surprise to me because I had been losing a great deal of blood through my urine for several days. He told me that the transfusion would alleviate a plethora of problems and assured me it would be quite safe. I totally trusted him and was not worried in the least. My relationship with worry had all but disintegrated, and fear was having a very difficult time rattling my cage over much of anything.

After I received the transfusion, I was quite calm, and we were settling in for the night. Somehow, a thought came to me that I had not made out a list of where important items were kept in my apartment. Everything was in very good order, but no one would know exactly where all of this good order was. This greatly disturbed me because a friend who had passed away awhile back left behind an impossible treasure hunt. I was not about to leave a confused mess for my survivors. I made Paula get out of bed, and we spent the next hour going through the locations of all the important items. I could see this was beginning to make her uncomfortable, but she begrudgingly did an excellent job at dictation. I explained that having things in the best possible order would allow me to remain free of any worry or stress for tomorrow's surgery. Although the doctors were very optimistic, we were warned that the unexpected could still occur. Once we finished, I was able to drift off into a restful sleep and slept soundly through the night.

The Surgery Zone!

The following morning, I woke up later than I expected. The surgeon appeared in my room to report that he was postponing the operation for a few hours. I asked him why, and he said he wanted to give the transfusion more time to settle in my body. He decided it would be best to go into surgery sometime in the afternoon. He insisted that a few more hours would make a big difference. Surprised, I said, "Can you just cancel like that?"

He replied, "I can do whatever I like if I think it best. We can wait until tomorrow if need be."

I told him that I hoped that was not necessary because I was really ready to do this today. He laughed and told me not to give it another thought. He assured me that it would happen before the end of the afternoon. He stated that all I needed to do was remain calm and relaxed.

So, we waited. Now, I really needed to step into action and apply my Alexander principles big time. This was an extremely challenging feat because I had already been without food for nearly 24 hours and I was verging on madness. Luckily, I was saved just a bit before 1 pm when the doors of the room burst open and an entire team of people entered with a large gurney. Things moved with lightning speed because the window of opportunity was wide open. I was never so grateful in my life to be cut open. They could have driven a stake through my heart, and I would have been just as happy. The first person I met when I arrived to surgery was the anesthesiologist. He explained everything he was about to do to me in perfect English. This came as a great relief because the hunger was impeding my ability to translate. He then went ahead and gave me the first injection, and from then on, I slipped into what I call the surgical zone.

I had been through the joys of surgery once before when I was 15 years old for a ruptured appendix. During that entire operation, I felt as though I was suspended in a very dark empty place. There was no pain, no fear, no anxiety, or thought of any kind. There was just a sense of being suspended in a void of dark timelessness that left me with the impression that I had been floating in outer space. When I awoke from my appendectomy, I was writhing in excruciating pain with my hands restrained. The pain was so agonizing that I thought I was being tortured to death. Astoundingly, this surgical experience was identical to my first one except when I awoke, I thought I had died and gone to heaven. To encapsulate it in one word: Nirvana.

Is That a Nurse?

In my first moments of consciousness, I thought that the operation had not even taken place because I felt so utterly spectacular. Down by the bottom of the bed, I noticed a rather glamorous woman. She struck me as out of place, and I could not figure out why she was standing there looking at me. I called to her because I thought perhaps she was a nurse, but there was no response. On the other side of the room was a man at a desk who was occupied with something. I called out to him and he also gave no response. I was perplexed and wondered if this was really happening or not. I scrunched up the sheet that covered me with my hand, and the sensation of it felt real. I looked back at the woman to call to her once again, and to my utter amazement, I realized that she was my grandmother. Now, I was beyond confused.

She seemed to be as real as everything else, and yet how was this possible? What was going on? She appeared grander and more glamorous than my grandmother had ever been during her life or in my recent dreams. I was certain that I must be wrong. Maybe it was someone else who resembled her or simply reminded me of her; however, as I continued to gaze at this lovely apparition, I was absolutely sure that it was indeed my grandmother. With this thought of certainty, she began to silently speak to me. I use the word silently because she did not speak in words per se, but through a kind of transmission that seemed to pour out of her. This transmission seemed to deliver a very clear and poignant message, but astoundingly, I could not understand a word of what she was saying. It was absolutely mind-boggling.

It suddenly dawned on me that perhaps I am dead. This thought made me strangely giddy; it was as though this was the best thing that could happen to me at this moment. I instantly had no care or concern in the world but felt freed from it. Suddenly, I became aware of having extreme thirst, and I called out for water. My grandmother simply smiled at me while the man at the desk finally turned and looked at me. He asked me what was wrong. I told him that I was thirsty and wanted some water. He explained that I would have to wait until I was back in my room. His response brought me to the realization that I was absolutely alive and that the surgery was over. With this new understanding, I looked back over at my beautiful grandmother to tell her that I was alive, and she had simply vanished. How could that be? She seemed to have been there for so long, and now she was gone. I deeply regretted requesting the water. My momentary distraction of thirst had cruelly snatched her out of my life once again.

My Triumphant Return

The time to go back to my room had arrived, and a group of attendants assembled to assist. I was so happy to be in their presence because they all appeared to be so beautiful and loving. I began to talk to them a mile a minute. I felt triumphant and jabbered away about all kinds of nonsense. As I entered the room, I saw my sister's smiling face and began telling her how wonderful and amazing I felt. She responded with a rather worried and perplexed look. I asked her what was wrong. Her face grew more anxious as she gasped the word, "English." I could not understand what she meant by this. I ran the word through my mind, but I could not seem to figure out what in God's name she was trying to tell me. She grew even more distressed when I told her that I had no idea what she was talking about. Once again, she shouted the word, "English!" and all at once, the meaning of the word hit my consciousness, and a cascade of English began to pour from my mouth. As unbelievable as it was to me, I had been speaking in Spanish the entire time. I could have sworn I was speaking in my native tongue.

Paula was immediately relieved by my return to the English shores and erupted with the news that the surgery was a total success. It had gone better than anyone expected. This news immediately prompted me to have her make a call to the Neighborhood Playhouse. I am not exactly sure why, but I deeply needed to speak to them at that precise moment. Lo and behold, everyone was still there, and I finally managed to get Pamela on the line. My euphoric babbling continued, and she must have thought I had gone stark raving mad. She said how happy she was to hear the news and thanked me for the call. She also cautioned me to please take care of myself, and get some rest. I am sure she must have thought that I was drugged to delirium and might try to fly out of a window. I agree that the drugs contributed enormously to my heightened state of madness, but this euphoria seemed to go beyond that. My sister took over the call, and I am sure explained everything much more coherently than I could have ever done. I continued dealing with nurses and attendants who were now setting me onto my bed with various contraptions that I was hooked up to. I also was begging for water and received a large delightful cup of ice that was worth its weight in gold.

As the buzz of activity slowed down after what seemed to be an eternity, silence descended. I had been running the events of the recovery room repeatedly through my mind so as to keep them fresh in my memory. Finally, my sister and I were alone, and it was my chance to reveal every detail of what had happened. I went through it very carefully and reported everything just as it had unfolded. By the end of it, Paula was in awe and completely speechless. She was as shocked as I was that our grandmother had made yet another appearance in such a strange and mysterious guise. We were both bewildered as to its possible meaning.

Angels Unite

I was also interested to hear what had been going on with Paula while I was in surgery. She said that she had been on the phone a lot and reported that she had received texts concerning the psychic work Debbra Gill was doing and the prayer circle. Anne Waxman later reported that her hands were buzzing with energy. Everyone in the circle seemed to have had a very positive experience, and I believe that it added to the success of the surgery; although, God knows we would never be able to prove that one in a court of law. Paula was deeply touched when the surgeon called her toward the end of surgery. He knew that she was alone, and he could not get a message in English to her easily, so he decided to slip away and let her know how wonderfully it had gone. She added that he was blown away with how easily the tumor was removed and would later state that it "came out like a baby." I was elated with this particular phrase because this is exactly how I had envisioned my tumor almost from the beginning. One time, I had the whole dining room laughing hysterically over my miraculous baby that I was giving birth to, but I had never mentioned any of this to the surgeon. All these wonderful things were happening, as my body lay unconscious on the operating table and all of them aimed at saving my life. I was immensely grateful for the love, care, and concern that had been heaped onto me at such a precarious moment in my life. It was as though I had 12 legions of angels at my service heralding me through to victory and awaiting my return home.

I was still hopped up and did not tire. I very much wanted to go back through all the details about what I had witnessed in the recovery room with Paula. We went through every detail again and began to examine the similarities and differences in my grandmother's various appearances. The dreams were a good representation of how I actually remembered her in life, although she was a bit more youthful and angelic. In the recovery room, however, she was nearly unrecognizable and filled with celestial serenity. She reminded me of a very glamorous movie actress who was starring as a saint. I intuitively sensed there was a clue hidden in these differences that could possibly unlock something important to this mystery. It both fascinated and confounded me because I could not decipher it. Besides, what in God's name was she saying to me, and why did I not understand it? What was blocking me? No matter how much I tried to unravel this mystery, I did not have an inkling as to what it was all about.

Grandma's Encore

Once the excitement wore off and I had exhausted my mind over the contemplation of grandma, I became very tired. Paula and I had more excitement in one day than either of us ever thought possible, so we went to sleep. While I slept, I slowly became aware that I was mysteriously back in the deep void of the surgical zone once again. I could not fathom what was happening. I struggled to convince myself that the surgery was over. I awoke suddenly with a gasp so loud that my sister immediately sprang to my bedside and cried out, "What's wrong? Should I send for the nurse?"

"No, I am fine. I know what Grandma Ramsey said to me. She was thanking me for everything that I did for her, Dad, and Aunt Barbara."

"What? What are you talking about? That's crazy! What did you do for them? What did she say?"

"The surgery!"

"But, Gar, that does not make any sense."

"I know!" I replied. "But that is what she said. I had given them all a great gift by going through the surgery. She told me that they all loved me, and they would be eternally grateful to me for what I have done."

Like a shot, the entire message had practically downloaded into my conscious mind the instant I woke up from the second surgery zone. We both sat there stunned and amazed once again by this latest news flash. It did not make logical sense. How could my surgery over here have done something over there for my family? Are we living in some sort of virtual game where actions over here score points over there? Why did I not understand the message in the recovery room? Was I still unable to grasp English at that point in time? Was all this just the effects of the anesthesia or simply a creation of my subconscious mind? None of it was clear to me nor did it make any sense whatsoever. There were so many unanswered questions and so much that was still unknown about my prognosis and recovery. One thing, however, was crystal clear to me: All these events were as real to me as anything else I have experienced in my life. Whether they were some concoction created in my mind or a chemical reaction from the drugs was irrelevant. For me, they were as real as every other experience, and all of it was beyond anything that I could have ever imagined. My past and present were colliding with each other, and the impact was immensely powerful and profound. I could not begin to comprehend where all of this would lead, but up to this point, the journey was already beyond my greatest expectation.

Chapter 9 – Making Sense of It All

Somewhere, something incredible is waiting to be known.

Sharon Begley

Salvation Ahead

It was over. I had survived the operation, and despite the sacrifice of my right kidney, I was in great shape. The sense of relief was nothing less than magnificent. Next on the agenda would be to deal with my cancer recovery. I had no idea what that would entail, nor did I care. Thus far, everything had gone beautifully, and I could not imagine that the universe would abandon me at this juncture. I had followed my intuition and inner guidance thus far, so why not continue? I felt like a prisoner who had been released from his tiny prison cell with nothing but freedom in front of him.

Early that morning, the nursing staff said that I could get up if I desired, and boy, did I ever. I was raring to go. I stood up as though I could conquer the world. I cannot even begin to tell you what was making me feel so wonderful: the drugs, the joy, the fact that it was over, or a combination of them all. Whatever it was, it kept me suspended on this overwhelming high. I went for a bit of a walk around my very large room, and it felt great. When I reported how terrific it was to be moving around, they asked me if I wanted to take a shower. I answered with an overwhelming, "Si!" I only needed assistance with my IV equipment and my drains to get into the shower. It was unbelievable to me that only a little more than 12 hours after surgery, I was this mobile. It was as though I was living a fairy tale, and I didn't have to deal with any of the wicked witches or the terrifying dragons. Paula and I remained at the hospital for the entire day. I felt bad for her because she was basically trapped in the room without much to do. She managed to keep busy with calls and correspondence while, I on the other hand, appreciated the down time. The day was spent relaxing, reading books aloud, writing, and answering e-mails. The big crisis was over, but I sensed that my life was about to transform into something unfamiliar.

The following morning, we were back on our way to the facility. The surgeon and the hospital staff were very happy with my progress and agreed that there was no reason for me to remain at the hospital. A car was arranged for Thursday morning, and we arrived at the front door of the facility by the early afternoon. As I walked into the lobby, there was a huge round of applause and a multitude of hugs coming from all who were in attendance. I was thrilled to be back and on the road to recovery. We spent the rest of that day relaxing by the ocean and enjoying the wonderful views.

When I saw the doctor the next day, he informed me that from what they could see during the surgery, I was cancer-free. This seemed very odd to me, and I asked how they could possibly have known that. I had always heard how cancer spreads and the painstaking treatments afterwards. They explained that I did not lose one drop of blood during the surgery (they refer to this as a "bloodless surgery"), and that they saw no evidence of the cancer spreading. They added that my tumor and my kidney were taken to a lab to be broken down to create a special serum for me. This serum was designed to kill any microscopic form of the cancer that may still be roaming around my body and bloodstream. It would also vaccinate me against getting this particular form of cancer ever again.

I thought they were joking at first, but in fact, they were not. For many years, they have been using these vaccines created from a patient's individual tumor. The serum attacks and kills only the cancer from which it was created, so it cannot be mass-produced. I found out that this sort of cancer treatment had been there for nearly 15 years and has been used in Germany for far longer. I marveled at all of this and could not believe what I was being told. There was to be no chemotherapy or radiation and no nasty side effects. I was in utter disbelief. It seemed as though I had travelled to the future where cancer treatments are kind and benevolent.

My healing continued to progress rapidly. Within three days, all drains had been removed, and not long after, my stitches were gone as well. I can only attribute all of this to the excellent care, the organic food, the herbal supplements, the continued oxygen treatments, Vitamin C drips, and the gorgeous environment I was surrounded by. My appetite had completely returned to normal, and I was slowly able to gain weight. I felt positively plump when I hit 144 pounds. My body fat, which had gone down to a shocking four percent, was now on the rise as well. I was allowed to workout in the walking pools once again, provided that I did not get the wound wet. I was feeling so well and gaining so much strength that there was little need for my sister to remain with me any longer.

We had been having a wonderful time, and after the surgery, it became more like a vacation than anything else. Paula was enjoying herself, and we were finally able to really relax. Day by day, we received nothing but good news. I truly had found my paradisiacal fantasy island hospital and had my rapid recovery as proof. Though the $100/day cost for Paula to stay with me was miniscule, the demand to return to her not-so-miniscule 12-year-old daughter, Jade, won out. She went on her way, thrilled with all of the results and amazed by the entire experience. We said our goodbyes, and she was driven back through the gates to the San Diego Airport.

The Past Revisited

With Paula gone, I began to think more and more about why all of this happened to me. I developed a nagging need to know how my kidney became so sickened and destroyed. As odd as it may sound, I was grieving the loss of it. The image that kept coming to mind was that I had been some sort of sacrificial lamb for my paternal family. But why? Grandma's message still made no sense to me, and I continued to be dumbfounded by it. The whole scenario was surreal, and I was still in disbelief about how effortlessly everything had fallen into place after my diagnosis. The whole thing had the sense of being staged or set up. It all was suspect and had the underpinnings of some great orchestrator behind the scenes making magic appear before my very eyes. I myself could not believe half of it, and I began to wonder what was really going on.

Surprisingly, one answer to some of these questions surfaced relatively quickly. After the lab's examination of my kidney, the reports stated that I had once sustained a forceful impact on my right side. When the doctors first told me this information, I had all but forgotten an incident nearly 40 years before. They saw that my lumbar spine was permanently torqued a bit to the left due to an impact I received on my right side. I had been injured while unloading lumber from a very large moving truck on a summer theatre lot. Somehow, the safety ties had come undone, and when I went to take the next piece of wood, a large cascade of it fell on top of me. I landed on my left side with my upper torso protected near the wheel well of the truck, while the lower part of my torso and legs were crushed. Miraculously, I did not sustain any broken bones, but I had "bruised" many of them, or at least that is what I was told. I was advised to use crutches because my knees and pelvis were very sore. I recovered and did not think much about it until two years later when I began having back trouble.

The doctors were pretty certain that this accident had weakened my right kidney and probably led to its eventual demise. I learned from them that many cancers are able to slowly develop from impact or trauma to the body. I had never heard of this theory before, and yet it made sense to me. Shortly after the accident occurred, I began to experience a series of back and hip difficulties that went on for many years. These chronic problems also contributed to my study and certification in the Alexander Technique. This new information helped to alleviate my curiosity a bit, but there was still a nagging uneasiness that persisted.

I soon discovered from other lab results that my remaining kidney was becoming very distressed. I learned that this is not uncommon after a nephrectomy because the remaining kidney has no idea what happened to its partner. It was a bit of a setback because I needed to remain at the facility longer than expected. I was concerned whether my bank account would be overburdened because the cost would now go over the estimated one. I was confidant, however, that everything would work out financially, and in the end, it more than did. I wanted to return to the States as healthy as possible, and I certainly did not want to be running back to Mexico for more treatments. I, therefore, remained an extra 13 days to complete the program.

My left kidney caught on quickly to the fact that it was now a lone star and responded very well to the treatments. During this time, I was struck by some interesting facts about the kidneys: They are twin organs, the purifiers of all fluids in the body, and only one of them is dominant and works at a higher capacity. Coincidently, I too am a twin, born under the water sign of Pisces. I am also the dominant twin in terms of personality traits while my twin brother, George, tends to be less dominant. Oddly enough, I happen to be dominant on the right side of my body, while George is dominant on his left. I found these parallels unusual and ironic. My remaining kidney was now my left non-dominant one while my right dominant one was removed and lost its place of power. These surprising discoveries led me to contemplate the concepts of dominance versus passivity within our world.

We all know that the flower appears more outwardly passive while the bee is busy buzzing around. I realized that this does not make either of them greater or lesser in any way because each of them creates a perfect union with the other. United they contribute to a far bigger result than either of them could accomplish in separation. I began to analyze my own relationship with George and how we countered each other to create a perfect balance between us. Though I may have outwardly appeared to be the busy one, he held inner abilities that were equally as powerful. In addition, now in the absence of my right dominant kidney, the left, less dominant one was stepping up to the plate and saving my life. I was fascinated by this ebb and flow of energy that constantly goes on around us. This continuous dance of energies creates a perfect unity in our current dualistic concept of reality. In fact, if the opposites do not create compatibility, there will be dissonance between them. I believe that this dissonance is what led to my illness in the first place. Though the accident may have been a catalyst, I believe that my desperate need to control my world at my own expense was the true dormant volcano waiting to erupt.

More and more, I saw the harmony and balance at work within my entire cancer scenario. It had actually come to me as my savior and not as my nemesis. It came to protect and prevent me from destroying myself. Practically every aspect of my cancer journey had brought startling and surprising revelations that uplifted my soul and spirit. The compassion and understanding that I now embodied, not only toward others but toward myself, had increased by tenfold. It also taught me to become more discerning in the world that I inhabited and to find balance and harmony within every moment. My whole comprehension of the universe was transforming into a kinder and more unified model rather than the old "survival of the fittest" mentality.

The deeper I dove into this new perspective, the more I saw the parallels between life/death and health/disease. First of all, they are never at odds with each other but rather at one with the whole spectrum that lies between them. We could say one of them is more active while the other is less active. For example: Hot is the absence of cold, but still has an element of cold within its structure; otherwise, it could never become hotter. They are intrinsically united because one would not exist without the other. The harmony and balance between them is crucial to their independent existence and must be honored. If not, an imbalance will reap havoc. My imbalance manifested in the form of attempting to manipulate and control my outer reality by assuming my role as a caretaker. The origins of this began very early in my development and originated in my relationship with my twin brother.

I worked at double the capacity to make up for what I mistook to be George's lack. My caretaking addiction also contributed to the development of my workaholic tendencies. I was never able to see beyond my misinterpretation because I perceived it as normal behavior. This dis-eased view of my reality continued to grow throughout my childhood until my entire perceptual reality saw caretaking and workaholism as the only means of survival. Seeing the kidneys as twins helped to awaken this parallel connection with my childhood so much so that I could barely grasp the enormity of it all. Cancer had literally paved the way for a major renovation of my conscious perceptual reality and woke me up beyond what I could have possibly imagined. It felt as though once my volcano of control erupted, my molten mind had been unleashed and flowed outwards to create a new matrix of reality for me to inhabit.

I was no longer sure of anything and was not certain what would happen when I arrived home. My work, my opera singing, and even my relationships all hung in the balance without the slightest sense of which way the proverbial pendulum would swing. Astoundingly, for one of the first times in my life, I was not the least bit concerned by any of it. I was released from my matrix of control and freed from the fears of my former self. I knew that I had changed forever and was not about to live another second with any concern about the future. To even attempt to do this felt sacrilegious in light of what I had been through.

As my departure date neared, I was scheduled to have a session with a practitioner of a technique called The Body Code. I had one of these sessions before my surgery, and I found it very interesting. I was not entirely sure how the technique worked, but my first session was very pleasant and left me feeling more balanced. There was a new practitioner named Susanne Weiss who had recently arrived, and I was scheduled to have this post-surgery session with her. When I met her at the front desk, we immediately hit it off. She said that they did not have my file because it had not been translated into English as of yet, and I would have to tell her a bit about myself. I told her that was fine and that I had some idea of what to expect from the previous session.

Shortly after we began, she asked my purpose for coming to the facility, and I simply said that I had surgery. By this time, I had grown very tired of recounting my extensive tale. She did not ask for details and confided that the less she knew, the cleaner her energy would be. During the reading, she became interested in one particular aspect of it that kept appearing over and over again. Finally, she said that we needed to go into an area called "spiritual heredity." I wanted to know exactly what that term meant. I had never heard it before and immediately the word "heredity" caught my attention. She explained that we not only inherit our physical traits but our spiritual ones as well. I was fascinated by this concept. She went on to say that something in my spiritual heredity wanted to make itself known for some reason.

She looked at me and said that an issue was coming from my paternal side, and it was passed down to me from my father's mother. I thought I would fall out of my chair. I simply could not believe it. I had not uttered one word about the dreams or the apparition to anyone other than my sister. She added that this heredity was passed on to my grandmother from her father. This was even more shocking because I knew that the two of them had a very close relationship with each other. My grandmother had lived with my great-grandfather and cared for him until his death.

I said nothing. I was still trying to comprehend all of this while she continued. She said the essence of this heredity was centered on the aspect of fear and hopelessness. It had been spiritually passed down for generations in my family tree. This not only described some of them to a tee but also the situation I had been thrown into at my diagnosis. She told me very emphatically that my grandmother was a gifted woman and seemed to know a lot about these kinds of things. She could see that my grandmother had the ability to clear this heredity by herself, but unfortunately, something went terribly wrong, and she died before accomplishing this. Prior to her death, she passed it on to me because I was the best possible choice.

She then asked me, "How old were you when your grandmother died?"

"Seven," I replied.

"Oh my word! She must have been very desperate indeed to have passed this on to one so young. It looks as though she knew what she was doing, however, because this heredity has been cleared."

I felt as though I had been shot out of a cannon that had scattered me into pieces everywhere. Slowly the pieces were descending into places on life's puzzle board. The dreams, my grandmother's appearances throughout my illness, and the message she had brought me were all harmonizing themselves into a masterful work of art. With my mind still swirling, Susanne asked, "What was your surgery for?"

"Kidney cancer," I replied.

Surprised, she said, "Symbolically, kidneys represent fear. Are you better?"

"Yes, they tell me that I am cured," I replied. "But I did have to lose the right kidney."

"You lost it?" she gasped. "Oh my goodness! Well, as far as I am concerned, not only has this heredity been cleared, it has been completely removed just as your kidney was."

"I'll drink to that! But, damn it, I can only drink green tea!" I shrieked.

We both began to crack up and soon roared with laughter. The whole thing seemed utterly ridiculous. How insane life is. At that moment, it seemed as though I had been sent on a journey in search of the golden goose. Yet, at the same time, I felt as though I had achieved something verging on the miraculous. I didn't care whether anything that I had just learned was true or not. In that moment, it was my truth. My past and present were one with everything that ever was and will ever be. From that little seven-year-old boy in the parking lot waving goodbye to his beloved grandmother, straight through to this moment of sheer laughter in Mexico with a woman who I barely knew—all aspects of me, from my past and future selves, seemed to be sitting before me in this present one. Words fail me as I write this. All I know is that I saw the sheer game of it all, and I marveled at its cleverly disguised brilliance. It all seemed to make perfect sense to me, and at the same time, it seemed perfectly senseless. I was filled with joy, laughter, and the thrill of the roller-coaster ride that I had been on. It was and continues to be a spectacular moment in the life and times of Gary Ramsey. It is one that I am privileged to have experienced, and I will never forget it for as long as I live.

Chapter 10 – Bliss

In the time of your life, live - so that in that wondrous time you shall not
add to the misery and sorrow of the world, but shall smile to the infinite
delight and mystery of it.

William Saroyan, The Time of Your Life

Countdown to Re-entry

After The Body Code session with Susanne, my current existence felt as though it had shifted into some other unknown reality. Although it was not very unlike my previous one, my life prior to cancer seemed so utterly absurd and trivial to me that it was laughable. I was not exactly sure where to go from here. Everything continued to flow perfectly toward my anticipated departure date. I noticed that I had a newfound love for what I formerly perceived as the mundane and the insignificant. Even a minor occurrence could produce a profound sense of gratitude flowing through my being. Every day was filled to the brim with final treatments, travel arrangements, and farewells. In the clinic's auditorium, I gave a final demo and lecture on the Alexander Technique and how I used its principles to help me through my illness. This was the last of a series of talks that I gave—all of them prompted by my amazing recovery.

My remaining days in Mexico came to an end without incident. As promised, my job was waiting for me as soon as I was ready to return to work. In addition, a dear friend of mine, Kathleen Kelly Sordelet volunteered to pick me up from the airport and insisted that I spend a couple of days at her home to acclimate myself. Everywhere I turned, everything seemed to be once again organizing itself perfectly without much help from me. This further demonstrated to me how much my life had radically altered and that it would never be quite the same again. I was beginning to become accustomed to this new sense of reality and as with everything else, simply accepted it.

PHOTO 6: GARY & ANITA MOORJANI; GARY & FRIENDS - RETURN TO USA (OCT 12, 2015)

I arrived in New York on October 10, 2015, and was back to work four days later. My entire journey came to a total of 48 days from the date of my diagnosis until the date of my return; just one day short of seven weeks. Things continued to unfold in the same magical and miraculous of ways. I basically stepped into the remnants of my old life and felt as though I had never been there before. The way I ate, slept, worked, and existed had completely transformed. My life now contained a formerly unnoticed splendor and wonder that I only had a glimpse of before my diagnosis. Whatever circumstance or challenge I encountered appeared to be a virtual illusion with no worry, struggle, or strain attached to it. I simply moved through each one of them easily and effortlessly without much care or concern. I saw everything as a lovely gift that I was being generously offered. I also saw the past as something filled with countless blessings that wove into the fabric of my present and paved the way for a glorious future. Within a few weeks, it was clear to me that life would never be the same again. This incredible high did not diminish in strength but grew stronger and more palpable instead.

I had the sense of having died and gone to heaven. Though I did not have a near-death experience like my hero, Anita Moorjani, it felt like I had. My entire concept of myself seemed to have simply vanished. No matter where I looked for it, I could not find it. All that remained was a boundless sense of total acceptance. Whatever happened simply happened. I was freed from the confines of need or want and ready to embark on whatever journey lay ahead of me with great abandon. After my return, the one question that people kept asking was: How did I get such a happy and blissful ending to my unhappy and grim story? I do not have a definitive or comprehensive answer to this rather simple question. I doubt if anyone will ever be able to figure it out. There are some people who have deemed my story as incredible, mundane, delightful, ridiculous, implausible, inspiring, pure nonsense, captivating, and plain bullshit. More and more, I understand that none of this is of any concern to me. The more important point to my entire odyssey was the journey itself.

Heroic Journey?

I have been a long-time fan of Joseph Campbell who was a leading authority on mythology and religion and their effects on the human psyche. Campbell's work was heavily influenced by Carl Jung, and in it he theorized that all myths are variations of a single great story called the Hero's/Heroine's Journey. He described it in this way: "A hero ventures forth from the world of common day into a region of supernatural wonder: fabulous forces are there encountered, and a decisive victory is won: The hero comes back from this mysterious adventure with the power to bestow boons on his fellow man." (Campbell, 1956)

For me, one of the primary points of Campbell's theory is that each and every one of us is living the hero's journey. I also agree that we are all heroes transcending challenges within our lives, and once we slay our dragon, we can return to a more expanded expression of our former world. I believe that our true journey begins only when we dare to enter the depths of our inner selves. There lies the potential to enrich our lives while traveling through places we have never been before. The external world will only reflect what we have accomplished in our internal one, and all possibilities and potentials are created there first. Many surprises may frighten us along the way or give us cause to pause or stop, but if we simply trust the journey itself and our inner guidance to the best of our abilities, we will uncover unknown treasures beyond our wildest dreams.

I would like to add that during my entire illness, I never saw myself as a hero nor did I see any of what happened as supernatural at the time. Only now am I able to see the uncanny parallel between Campbell's definition and my own experience. I did indeed "venture forth from the common way" and landed in a place that was certainly amazing, if not "a region of supernatural wonder." What "boons" then do I have to bestow on my fellow man? I can only answer with a phrase that Campbell repeatedly echoed in his interviews and writings, "Follow your bliss."

I religiously followed this advice and took it to heart during my illness. I only did those things that brought me joy, solace, and serenity. On my return, some people saw my actions as heroic while others thought me a foolish coward. I understand both points of view, although neither of them is completely correct. It would be more accurate to say that I had a burning desire to follow my intuition and was deeply compelled to do so. There were no thoughts of becoming anything or accomplishing something unless the moment inspired me to take action. I had no agenda other than to follow my bliss and to fully embrace and meet the demands of each moment along the way. The Yellow Brick Road I was on effortlessly appeared before me and led me to a clearer and brighter reality. I was very pleased with the results of my journey, and since I alone was the only one to have suffered and enjoyed the consequences of it, no other opinion is of any relevance.

Following one's bliss is a rather simple task to accomplish unless of course the person has no sense of what that might be. In many matters, we crowd out our bliss because we are taught to utilize our heads and intellects instead of our hearts and souls. Some of us also tend to feel safer doing what we are told to do rather than what we would like to do. We honor the opinions of others whom we deem as experts and/or those who appear wiser and more experienced. We do this largely because we have been conditioned to believe that they must surely know much more than we do. This is not necessarily true. Experts and the like are just as limited in their knowledge and their own perceptions as anyone else. Every single being will inevitably meet his or her own limitations because he or she can only contain and maintain so much information and ability, unless of course he or she is able to rise to what some consider higher states of consciousness. Even a genius can be just as stymied as anyone else about what he or she or someone else should or should not do. We are the only ones who truly know ourselves intimately enough to best decide what we can and cannot abide. We hold within us all the true genius that we will ever need during our entire lifetime—if we can but only gain access to it.

In addition to following our bliss, I also know that we need to remain free from the noise of our former beliefs that bar us from moving forward. Everything we encounter must be met head on with a fearless attitude toward the past or the future. Nothing else is of any relevance other than the sacredness of the present moment. This is the only sanctuary that truly matters. Examining the woes, whys, and wherefores of the past or future only diminishes the courage and tranquility necessary to continue our present journey. We are the deciding factor of the equation and write our entire scenario. We give form and action to the story and hold the key to the tale's end; therefore, why not walk fearlessly through our darkest hour into the light that illuminates our brightest future? Then and only then may we truly be free.

My Afterlife Rearranged

News spread of my renewed state of health quickly. My diagnosing physician here in the States was even interested in seeing a copy of my Mexican pathology reports. He was equally impressed with my speedy recovery and said that my current results were excellent for someone who had two kidneys, much less one. Friends and strangers alike began to hear about my amazing recovery. Many people contacted me for help and advice concerning their own health crises. My response would always be the same: follow your bliss. Since my return, I now see all healing in a very different light. I know that much of it depends on the mindset of the one who is to be healed. I am not suggesting that we need to have a certain belief or think in a particular manner. In fact, we do not have to really follow anything other than to be intimately aware of the mindset that we already possess. Therein lies the key. What do I think? Am I one hundred percent behind what I am doing? Am I feeling good about it, or am I not? I know for certain that any hesitation or uneasiness about any of these questions will only lead to unhappy results. I now realize that the outer treatment is far less critical than the inner acceptance of it. I have also found that clinging to any particular outcome will prove detrimental to the healing process. For many people, this can be one of the greatest stumbling blocks.

Of course, we would all like a positive outcome concerning any matter relating to our health and well-being, but sometimes this intention is of an egoic and/or idealistic nature. To be continuously healthy and free from death is not only absurd but it is ultimately unrealistic. Even if we can achieve a relatively illness-free life, death will certainly come knocking in the end. What I am certain of is that we need to follow our own unique path to capture our best of all possible worlds. Attempting to bypass our inner self is like gambling when we are broke; it will only lead to disastrous results. The best course of action lies deeper within our own creative source and is there for the taking, if we truly can become one with it. The quickest way to accomplish this is by letting go of control and fear. It is the only solution.

Thou Shalt One Day Die

Owning our vulnerability to illness and our ultimate inescapable dance with death helps to alleviate the fearful doom and gloom that surrounds them. It is our attempt to escape from them that leads to doomier and gloomier fears. We become fugitives on the run from our own unavoidable fate. I found that by embracing life and death at every moment, I was led to a deeper understanding of the magnificent oneness between them. Neither of them exists independently of each other but rather coexists as a glorious balanced unity at every instant. Even the passing of one moment to the next is the dance of life and death played out before us; as one moment dies, the next is born. Once we see through this delusion of separateness between the two, we have a greater chance to live happier and healthier lives. We do this by confidently accepting our fate and believing that it will always work toward a wonderful but unknown ending that is perfect for our personal evolution. By employing death as a potential mate, I was able to alleviate my fears of him on this wild sojourn and it made all the difference.

My Personal Resurrection

I apply these principles as my life continues to unfold in strange and mysterious ways. I have no idea what the future will bring nor does it concern me anymore. I follow my bliss and venture forth without a care in the world. My bliss now seems to arrive at my door spontaneously. Examples of this could potentially fill another book, but I will only give a few highlights to the reader.

I received a notice that Anita Moorjani would be speaking at the Omega Center in Upstate New York. It happened to be on a weekend that I was able to attend. By coincidence, during the workshop a topic came up regarding a situation similar to mine, and I raised my hand to respond. Anita and the entire room were struck by my story, and she requested to see me afterwards. She immediately asked if I would be a guest on her radio show, and I happily agreed. The show was well received and aired repeatedly. Hundreds of people contacted me to thank me for sharing my story and found it inspirational, while others sought help and advice or had more questions to ask, all of whom inspired me to write this book.

I personally met and established a relationship with Debbra Gill who had psychically assisted my surgery. I used her services for a very tricky surgery concerning my cousin-in-law. Although he already had two failed surgical attempts to resolve his life-threatening issue, the third one assisted by Debbra was a winner. She continues to help me as well as others I have recommended to her.

A former student of mine, Natasha Stone, who manages Global Gods Web Design Solutions, was so moved by my situation that she took it upon herself to create a new website for me. This was to replace the one that I decided to let go of when I thought I would die. Tess Cacciatore, a long-time friend from college and co-founder of Global Women's Empowerment Network / GWEN Studios, has continuously encouraged, supported, and advised me to write my story. Diana Espinosa, another former student and friend, not only offered to edit this book, but is generously helping me to self-publish and promote it.

The blessings continuously keep coming.

A Dead Man's Epitaph

Everywhere I turn, things continually shift toward my greatest good. Possibly the most unbelievable gift of them all is a call that came in asking if I would be available to audition for the title role in Rigoletto. The company, Amore Opera, was looking to replace someone who had been cast in the role but suddenly had to drop out during rehearsals. This was above and beyond my wildest dreams because not only was this the opera I took to Mexico to be cremated with, but it was my first opera audition upon my return. After I sang Rigoletto's first aria, Pari siamo!, I was immediately offered the role. This moment was as surreal as the countless others that have happened since my diagnosis. I have been living an unfathomable dream that I still have not awoken from and am now fairly certain that I never will.

Opening night made me feel as though I truly had become Campbell's quintessential hero of the greatest adventure ever undertaken: My glorious cancer journey has changed my life forever. I was both the star and the creator of my own greatest show on earth. I played my Gary Ramsey role and my Rigoletto one with great abandon in life and onstage... I now know that by remaining vibrantly awake through every moment, I was able to transform myself from a dead man walking to a fairy tale come true. I had traversed the depths of the lowest lows and the highest highs and completely acknowledge the delight and difficulty that each of them offers.

PHOTO 7: "RIGOLETTO," TOP PHOTO- B. A. VAN SISE; BOTTOM PHOTOS- AMORE OPERA

When all is said and done or when the fat lady sings or perhaps when the cows come home, there is nothing else but the preciousness of the present moment. That alone is all we have and ever will have, no matter what else may materialize in our lives. Why worry about what will or will not happen next? If we accept that we can die at any minute, perhaps we may then be able to let go of death and vibrantly live the moment we have been given. We can finally sit back, relax, and enjoy the wonderful ride that we are all on. Who knows what amazing and supernatural events may take place and change our lives forever. You never know; we may even end up wondering as I did, how on earth did I end up so happily ever after?

Bliss

At the center of your being you have the answer; you know who you are and you know what you want.

– Lao Tzu

Acknowledgements

I would like to acknowledge all of the people in our lives who, like guardian angels, work to uplift and support us when we are in need. You are the true harbingers of love who will change our world into the paradise that it was meant to be.

Some of these angels are named in the pages of this book; however, many more are not mentioned but are of equal significance.

I would like to mention a few who continue to generously offer their love and support above and beyond the call of duty.

To Lulu Murphy at TheProofreaders.com for her precise and detailed work.

To the fans of Anita Moorjani who inspired me to write this book.

To Anita Moorjani for taking the risk to share my story with the world and generously endorsing this book.

To Anita's assistant Roz Brooks, who has tirelessly supported me through thick and thin.

To Colin Quinn for graciously accepting to write the forward of this book and for his outstanding faith in the work we have done together.

To my sister, Paula, who always seems to be there just when she is needed and never questions why.

And to Diana Espinosa, whose belief in my work and dedication to my story were vital components in bringing this book to fruition. Without her, it would have remained nothing more than a mere dream.

About the Author

At heart, Gary Ramsey is an eternal student of the universe, although he has been a teacher for much of his working career. Gary has walked many different paths that have taken many surprising twists and turns. Through it all, his love and compassion for all of mankind has continued to grow as well as his ability to live life artfully. He is honored to have worked and served in several different capacities throughout his lifetime.

Gary was born and raised in a blue-collar neighborhood in South Side of Chicago. Although his upbringing did not support higher education, he cleverly managed to attain a BFA in theatre from Stephen's College, an MFA in acting from Rutger's University, and a certification as an Alexander Technique teacher (ACAT). His interests grew in many different directions but solidified for him when he became a voice and speech teacher at the Neighborhood Playhouse School of the Theatre. There he was able to expand and grow both as a teacher and an artist. His continued vocal development led him to the operatic stage where again, he was able to further expand his performing and teaching abilities.

His life was filled with much happiness and great health until cancer struck in the summer of 2015. Since that experience, the core of Gary's reality was uprooted and tossed into yet another more perplexing and mystifying one. He emerged from this metamorphous into a world far greater than what he had previously known before and as a result lives life more vibrantly. He stands firm in the belief that within our own self lies the kingdom through which we will achieve our greatest glory here on earth.

Printed in Great Britain
by Amazon

84275177R00057